WITNESS TO LIFE

WITNESS TO LIFE

Preaching and Poetry as Theology and Art

CHARLES L. BARTOW

With an Essay and Poems by
Ernest Winfield Bartow

Foreword by
Clayton J. Schmit

RESOURCE *Publications* · Eugene, Oregon

WITNESS TO LIFE
Preaching and Poetry as Theology and Art

Resource Publications
An Imprint of Wipf and Stock Publishers
199 W. 8th Ave., Suite 3
Eugene, OR 97401

www.wipfandstock.com

PAPERBACK ISBN: 979-8-3852-2265-0
HARDCOVER ISBN: 979-8-3852-2266-7
EBOOK ISBN: 979-8-3852-2267-4

VERSION NUMBER 08/02/24

MEMORIAL DEDICATION

For Evans Crawford, Doris Gayle and all the saints known and unknown who have entered into their rest.

"Blessed are the dead which die in the Lord from henceforth: Yea, saith the Spirit, that they may rest from their labors; and their works do follow them" (Rev 14:13, KJV).

A TRIBUTE

On the occasion of the fiftieth anniversary celebration of
Dr. Crawford's contributions to theological education.

TO DR. EVANS E. CRAWFORD AND HIS WIFE, ELIZABETH

(Eph 1:11–14)

Let me join my aging voice
To those voices young and strong
That rightly sing your praises,
Preacher, teacher, dean—and friend
Even to the unfriendly
And to the "poor in spirit,"
Poor in worldly goods as well:
A man in Christ visioning
A world where no one's forlorn,
Or hounded, or unwanted,
And praying that world to be
Fervently, eloquently,
Your dear Elizabeth too,
With you and praying for you.
You are celebrated now
And will be celebrated
When all dreary, human hates
Are dead, laid to rest, and love's
Blest flames burn into the core
Of every last human soul
That gospel you preached, and prayed,
And lived, that with you, we all
Might be to God's praise and glory.

17 July 2010

Contents

Foreword

THE POET'S FIRST TASK is perception. "Those who have ears to hear," Jesus said, "let them hear." And eyes to see, we quickly comprehend. You cannot write of life or Life if you have not profoundly perceived it. Most everyone sees, but the poet is driven by some inner compulsion to see deeply, to record on some inner memory drive that which was once keenly seen; and then, when the *kairos* occurs, to recount what was seen for the sake of others who seek to know, to understand, to see what they have not seen for themselves—or what they have seen, but in a different light.

The poet's second task is selection. It's not an easy task, looking for the right word from out of the one hundred and seventy-thousand words available in English (according to the Oxford Dictionary). It is astonishing to me that poets, with all those words to choose from, usually select simple words. One rarely needs a dictionary at hand to read poetry. It is the common words that can burst with uncommon meaning. Metaphors are hand grenades thrown into sentences. They explode with meaning and every meaning, though vastly varied from one person to another, is potent and has the power to change the reader or listener. Similes are like flowers, chosen to brighten a textual bouquet. Selection, then, is critical. Poets adore words and love to employ their plasticity. Poets usually do this not for the sheer joy of euphony or syllabic fantasy (as Dr. Seuss has done so well). They do it because they are, like most artists, in service to the truth, the reality they have experienced and perceived. Poets who are followers of Christ do it so that we can meet whom they have met, understand what they have come to know, and believe the Truth, as they have known it, lived it, experienced it in their lives. They use words well so that we can have faith. Both poets and preachers do this.

This slim volume demonstrates this. These two poet-preachers have perceived, each through fourscore years, the joys and annoyances, the exultations and the exhaustions, the faith and the fears of lived experience. They have perceived all that life entails and have seen it honestly. They have also read of, studied, and lived the life of Christian faith. Chuck is a teaching theologian; Ernie is a preaching theologian. Each is committed to lifting up Christ in the face of human feeling. They have come to realize, as Suzanne Langer has taught, that art is the creation of expressive forms that symbolize human feeling and experience. Poetry, whether in the form of verse, prose, or preaching, has the capacity to speak to things that reside at the soul-deep level of human experience. Preachers and poets have come to understand this abiding paradox: they speak of things too deep for words—yet they succeed by using words. The words found here give profound "witness to life." They also witness to Life, as known in Christ.

The pages that follow contain the ordinary words of two graceful artists. The selection and setting of the words are extraordinary. Reading these lines stirs the imagination and beckons the reader in contemplation of things known and unknown, remembered, forgotten, suffered, celebrated, secreted, doubted, and believed. They speak of life in all its facets, of mortality, and above all, of Christ whose love makes immortality the longest, brightest, and most shimmering face of this hard stone that we call life.

Those who read these words without firm faith will find Christ in them, proclaimed and praised. They will resonate in the hearts of those who pray "Lord, help my unbelief." Those who read with faith alive will be graced with the kind of proclamation that is always needed by those who return to Scripture and worship for the ceaseless inspiration that Life in Christ provides.

These two brothers, these witnesses, are trustworthy. You are invited to read on, to see what they have seen, and to believe what they so convincingly believe.

Clayton J. Schmit
Epiphany, 2024

Preface and Acknowledgments

HIS LAST WORDS TO me were in a phone conversation. He said, "Chuck, trust the Bible." His name: Cullen I. K. Story, a colleague and friend of many years. Cullen was a biblical scholar whose commentary on the Gospel according to John titled *The Fourth Gospel: Its Purpose, Pattern, and Power*[1] was of enormous help to me in drafting the libretto for the opera *Resurrection*. That libretto is the fourth and concluding chapter of this book.

I do trust the Bible. It is the word of God written. It is *the* means of grace, along with other ordinary means—word as Scripture reading and preaching, sacrament, and prayer—by which God makes Godself known to us. To the Holy Scriptures we are bound if we would know God at all. The Bible also unfailingly, even infallibly, witnesses to human life as God intended it and intends it still. It also witnesses to what human life has become in this "present age" (*secularis profanus*, i.e., secular age), east of Eden. What we ourselves have made of the life given us by God clearly is not what God intended for it from the beginning. Therefore we await life in the "age to come" which life, in a prolepsis, already has dwelt or tabernacled among us in him who is life's Alpha and Omega, life's beginning and end (Rev 24:6). Our human future, along with the future of the natural environment within which we live, is vouchsafed to us in Christ Jesus. In Christ Jesus, as Karl Barth has written, we have *The Humanity of God*[2] disclosed to us.

---

1. Story, *Fourth Gospel*, 361–78.
2. Barth, *Humanity of God*, 11–33; 37–65.

My personal life journey through this present age has many more years behind it than ahead of it. I am what is called "old," no longer "young old" and not yet "old old," just plain "old." Regardless of my age, it is my hope that the contents of this book of sermons, poems, and an essay on the thought of lay theologian and societal critic, William Stringfellow, may be of use to readers in their own life and witness as they journey through this "present age" with heart and mind alert to intimations of the "age to come."

My brother, Ernest Winfield Bartow, at eighty-eight years of age, is two years older than I. His poems, however, in many cases clearly are addressed to a much younger generation. Furthermore, his poems, and his essay on Stringfellow, witness to life as it is—and is to be—with realism, vitality and urgency. His essay on William Stringfellow (based on his thesis for Princeton Theological Seminary) is taken from his diary, his love letter, so to speak, to his children and their children, Ernie's grandchildren and his great-grandchildren.

In Holy Scripture, the word for "witness" is "martyr." To give witness is to give life, to risk life, in service to the Life that is Life Indeed. The rightly celebrated Lutheran preacher and teacher of preachers, Dr. Paul E. Scherer, once said in my hearing, "You *will* give your life for something. The only question is for what and for whom." So with what I've got left of life in this present age, I give you, the reader, such a witness as I, along with my brother, Ernie, am able to make. And, in making it, I gladly sing, "Blessed assurance, Jesus is mine,"[3] but also, I sing, "Blessed disturbance, for I am His."[4] For the peace we have from God, which "surpasses all understanding" (Phil 4:7), is never mere peace and quiet at any price for anybody. It is disquiet with the world as it is and with ourselves as we are.

In writing and editing this book on preaching, poetry, and an essay by my brother, Ernie, I have drawn strength and encouragement from numerous sources across sixty years of local church pastoral ministry and university and seminary teaching. It clearly

---

3. Crosby, "Blessed Assurance," hymn 139.

4. Scherer, in my lecture notes and personal remembrance.

is impossible to list all those sources here. The sources I do list, then, must be the part that represents the whole. The Reverend Craig M. Barnes, PhD, erstwhile president of Princeton Theological Seminary, Academic Dean Jacqueline Lapsley, and the Princeton Theological Seminary board of trustees have provided deeply appreciated support for us faculty retirees. Joan Petrowski, of the Office of Academic Affairs, arranged many years of secretarial assistance for me. Meg Acer, office manager at First Presbyterian Church, Ramsey, New Jersey, has given me access to such technological knowhow as I myself sorely lack. Meg, with her daughter, Mika Chin, has prepared the final digitized text for this volume. Students of mine, and congregants of the churches I have served have helped me sharpen my thoughts and hone my skills with their honest words of encouragement and critique. The late Reverend Dr. Evans Crawford, emeritus dean of the Chapel at Howard University and professor of preaching at Howard Divinity School, has been, and remains, an inspiration to prayer and to service to the gospel of Christ Jesus, our Lord and Savior. To him especially, and to my former parishioner Doris Gayle, and to others who have died in the Lord, this book is dedicated.

Colleagues of mine in academies of the church have been unstinting in support of my research and teaching. Their constructive critical insights into my labors have ever been and remain treasured. These friends and colleagues include: Dr. Jana Childers, Newhall Professor of Homiletics and Speech Communication at San Francisco Theological Seminary, the Rev. Dr. Clayton J. Schmit, who generously offered to write the forward to this book, Dr. Nancy Lammers Gross and Dr. Michael Brothers of Princeton Theological Seminary, and Dr. Paul S. Undreiner, composer of the opera, "Resurrection," for which, at his request, I provided the libretto. Paul is director of music at First Presbyterian Church, Ramsey, New Jersey. The congregants of the Presbyterian Church of Deep Run, Bucks County, Pennsylvania, in the days of my pastorate there, and for many years thereafter, gave witness to life and to "art for faith's sake"[5] in the church and in the surround-

5. Schmit, "Art for Faith's Sake," 3–5.

ing community, especially through the Deep Run Festival of the Arts held annually for over twenty years. The festival raised funds for the inner-city, triracial mission at Temple Presbyterian Church in Philadelphia. The congregants at First Presbyterian Church, Ramsey, New Jersey, have made significant contributions in support of visual and performing arts and through their prayers and in their fellowship, I have found and continue to find nourishment for life and for witness to him who is "the way, the truth, and the life" (John 14:6).

My family all along has been supportive beyond my deserving. My brother, Ernie, at my request, has made his contributions to this book, his essay on Stringfellow and his poems. I am grateful for Ernie's contributions. My thanks to my daughters, Emma Ruth, Paula Sue, and Rebecca Jane, and their soulmates, James, Dino, and Darian. My thanks, also, to my grandchildren, Alexander, Tori, Miguel, and Mateo, in whom I rejoice daily.

My wife of fifty-nine years, Ruth Paula Goetschius Bartow, has typed much that I have written, starting with my master's thesis in religious television production for Michigan State University and my PhD dissertation in speech and homiletics for New York University. Paula also typed the manuscript for my first publication, *The Preaching Moment: A Guide to Sermon Delivery*.[6] Quite literally, Paula helps to keep me alive. And when it seems life's about to "tumble in"[7] somehow she finds a way to encourage me to "keep on keeping on." Her witness to life and to the Lord of life—and her sheer joy in living—is contagious.

Charles L. Bartow
Ramsey, New Jersey
1 September 2023

---

6. Bartow, *Preaching Moment*, 12.
7. Gossip, "When Life Tumbles In," 198–204.

CHAPTER ONE

THE LIVING WORD: SERMONS
Introductory Essay

PREACHING IS A SPOKEN word from the written word in witness to the incarnate Word, what a poet-theologian has called the *poesis* of God.[1] Therefore, let us turn to the written word of Holy Scripture, the wellspring of all attempts at preaching "the word of life" (Phil 2:16).

"In the beginning was the Word [*logos*], and the Word was with God, and the Word was God. He was in the beginning with God. All things came into being through him, and without him not one thing came into being. What has come into being in him was life, and the life was the light of all people. The light shines in the darkness, and the darkness did not overcome it" (John 1:1–5).

Preaching is a witness to the Life that is Life Indeed: in the world, yet not of it, in a given present moment, yet not held by the moment. Preaching is Holy Spirit led witness to Christ Jesus (the *logos*, the Word that was with God and was and is God, Christ crucified, risen, regnant). This ever living Word of God is present for us, *pro-nobis*, in Holy Scripture's attestation of him. And, with words freely chosen in an attempt by servants of the word[2] faithfully to speak what Scripture attests, the Word himself, Christ Jesus

1. Guite, *Faith, Hope and Poetry*, 60.
2. Farmer, *Servant of the Word*.

1

(the *Christus Praesens*)[3] is present, bearing witness to himself and to his Father, the only God who is "above all, and through all, and in all" (Eph 4:6). As I have elsewhere written, preaching is *God's Human Speech*.[4] Therefore, it is humble speech, prayerfully undertaken after the manner of him who "emptied himself. . . . And became obedient to the point of death—even death on a cross" (Phil 2:5–8). The witness to Christ in the Bible is meant to be heard; it is meant to be truly heard and felt, embodied: "[Let those with] ears to hear, hear" (Matt 11:15 KJV). Spirit-led listening, true to Scripture hearing, never is simply titillation of the eardrums. Likewise, the witness to life given us in Christ Jesus in preaching is meant to be heard, felt, embodied, that is, lived. Faith comes "by hearing and hearing by the word of God" (Rom 10:17 KJV). We can read of it in the Second Helvetic Confession: the preaching (and Holy Spirit hearing) of the word of God "is the word of God."[5] Preaching is Holy Spirit to human spirit speech: "God is spirit, and those who worship [God] must worship [God] in spirit and in truth" (John 4:24).

The sermons that follow have not been updated from the moment, time, and place of their original utterance. However, they attempt faithfully to proclaim the gospel—the Life that is Life Indeed—which transcends all limits of time and place. The holy gospel of our Lord Jesus Christ speaks to every moment and place, securing for itself a faith-filled listening and embodied hearing. The sermons that follow are offered "through faith for faith" (Rom 1:17).

---

3. Kay, *Christus Praesens*, 114.

4. Bartow, *God's Human Speech*, 1–7.

5. *Book of Confessions*, 5.004.

THE YOKE THAT BEARS THE BEARER UP

Text: Matt 11:28–30

> Come to me, all you that are weary and carrying heavy
> burdens, and I will give you rest. Take my yoke upon you,
> and learn from me; for I am gentle and humble of heart,
> and you will find rest for your souls. For my yoke is easy,
> and my burden is light.

"Come to me," Jesus said—we just heard him—"Take my
yoke upon you, and learn from me." "Learn what?" we might ask.
Why, learn "the way of God statutes," to use the words of the poet
in Ps 119. But why Jesus' yoke and not the yoke of God's law as
understood by its authorized and celebrated interpreters? Why
come to Jesus, that out-of-the-mainstream rabbi from out-of-
the-way Nazareth of all places? "Can anything good come out of
Nazareth?" (John 1:46). Even a truly guileless Israelite, Nathanael,
had to wonder. Why shouldn't we? Why come to Jesus instead of
to the teachers of the law whose credentials had been certified in
ancient Israel's synagogues—and in the temple at Jerusalem—for
generations?

Of course Jesus' uniqueness already had been noted in *how* he
taught God's word, God's law, "the way of God's statutes," concern-
ing which he said, "Not one letter, not one stroke of a letter, will
pass from the law until all is accomplished" (Matt 5:18). After what
is called his "Sermon on the Mount," we are told how the crowds
"were astounded at his teaching, for he taught . . . as one having
authority, and not as their scribes" (Matt 7:28). We note as well
that in his rebuke of his generation's unresponsiveness to either
John the Baptist's message regarding the nearness of the kingdom
of God, or his own message having to do with the same subject,
Jesus referred to himself as "The Son of Man" (Matt 11:19). "Son
of Man" is a messianic title taken from the book of Daniel where
it refers to a representative human figure "to whom universal and
everlasting dominion shall be given."[6]

---

6. Davis and Gehman, *Westminster Dictionary of the Bible*, 572.

Then, in climactic fashion, in the verse from Matthew's Gospel immediately preceding our text, Jesus spoke of himself as the unique Son of God in whom the presence of God and the will of God are made known. He said,

> All things have been handed over to me by my Father;
> and no one knows the Son except the Father, and no one
> knows the Father except the Son and anyone to whom
> the Son chooses to reveal him (Matt 11:27).

In other words, Jesus came as he said, not to abrogate the law or the prophets, but to fulfill them (Matt 5:17), and to invite you and me—and anyone else with ears to hear—to join him in his fulfillment of them. So there it stands, now as then; and either it is sheer chutzpa, an outrage, blasphemy, as those who sought to do away with Jesus found it (Matt 26:65), or it is an authentic divine invitation happily to be taken up. "Come to me," Jesus says to us now. Is it an option merely, or a self authenticating authoritative cancellation of all options save this one? "Take my yoke upon you and learn from me; for I am gentle and humble in heart."

Jesus said he is "gentle"; the word can be translated, has been translated, "meek." "Meek" does not indicate obsequiousness. It indicates that what pleases Jesus is not the pursuit of self-interest. Instead, what pleases him is to do what serves his Father's good pleasure, whatever the cost. And we know that at last, it cost Jesus himself dearly. Further, Jesus is long-suffering. That he is gentle implies that he is long-suffering as well as meek. So, for example, though Jesus never condones sin, he does forgive it. He bears patiently, urgently, yet patiently with sinners, even the worst, so that women, and men, and children as well, may feel the burden of sin (of rebellion against the way of God's statutes) lifted. Therefore, they are freed more and more to live beyond the debilitations of guilt. I've heard it claimed that he who controls the world's guilt controls the world.

But if sin is forgiven, if humanity's burden of guilt is lifted, guilt is no longer available as a means of control and humanity goes free. Humanity goes free to aspire to a standard of conduct that, in this life, it is unlikely to achieve: withholding anger when provoked, refraining from insult when insulted, holding out hope of reconciliation in the face of what may appear to be irreconcilable differences, seeking the total welfare of those who couldn't care less for you—who in fact may have "done you dirt"—which is what it means to love your enemies. All this is explicated in the Sermon on the Mount (Matt 5–7). Nineteenth-century poet Robert Browning caught the sense of it: "Ah, but a man's reach should exceed his grasp / or what's a heaven for?"[7] Jesus puts it in the plainest prose: "Be perfect . . . as your heavenly Father is perfect" (Matt 5:48). There's an earful! Jesus' gentleness, his meekness, his long-suffering must not be mistaken for an indulgent affection tolerant of everything that comes its way. Renowned mid-twentieth-century preacher George Arthur Buttrick called it a "hidden fire of wrath"[8] kindled to burn everything that encumbers people as they seek to be taught "the way of God's statutes, and observe it to the end" (Ps 119:33).

Then Jesus says he is "humble in heart." Likewise we—who should doubt it?—are instructed to be humble in heart, in will, in intention. We are to take Jesus' yoke upon ourselves, surrendering willfulness in self-regard as we undertake the life-work to which Jesus calls us. Jesus' humility is beautifully summed up in Phil 2, where the apostle Paul's epistolary prose trembles on the brink of poetry and song. There the apostle says of Christ Jesus that "though he was in the form of God," he

> did not regard equality with
>   God
>   as something to be exploited,
> but emptied himself,
>   taking the form of a slave,
>   being born in human likeness.
> And being found in human form,
>   he humbled himself
> and became obedient to the

---

7. Browning, "Andrea Del Sarto," 77.
8. Buttrick, *Interpreter's Bible*, 390.

point of death–
even death on a cross.
Therefore God also highly
exalted him
and gave him the name
that is above every name,
so that at the name of Jesus,
every knee should bend,
in heaven and on earth and
under the earth,
and every tongue should confess
that Jesus Christ is Lord,
to the glory of God the Father (Phil 2:5-11).

In Eastern Orthodox worship this ancient Christian hymn, held in mind as a single-word phrase, is sung while a liturgical cross is lowered and raised over worshippers in benediction to symbolize Christ's humiliation and glorification. Thus, through sung praise (and lived experience), Christ's humiliation and glorification are shared by all who believe in Jesus as the one—the *only* Son—whom the Father knows and who knows the Father, and who reveals the Father to whomever he chooses. And whom does he not choose?

To take upon oneself the yoke of Christ Jesus, then, is to seize upon Christ's invitation to become adopted daughters and sons of God, siblings of the only begotten Son of God (Rom 8:14–17). It is also to be joined to the true humanity of the messianic Son of Man as foretold by the prophet Daniel. Think of it! Our humanity joined to Christ's divinity through the Son of God's "entering this life of ours to bear himself the weight of it, forever merciful in his judgment, and just in all his compassion."[9] So it was put by the late, great Lutheran preacher and homiletician, Paul Scherer, my mentor, colleague and friend. The apostle Paul, in Colossians, startles us with these words: "You have died, and your life is hidden with Christ in God. When Christ who is your life is revealed, then you also will be revealed with him in glory" (Col 3:3b–4).

Can you take it in? Yoked to God's Son, we are not, by his Father—our Father—regarded as the morally compromised,

9. Scherer, "A Prayer," 333.

ethically obtuse, spiritually confounded, and guilt-burdened souls we from time to time—no doubt with warrant—may think ourselves to be. To the contrary, we are gentle, meek, long-suffering. We are humble, too, as he was humble, not in self-abnegation, but in self-fulfillment through service to God and neighbor. This staggers the imagination: we, you and I, by God, are counted among the humble, the gentle, the long-suffering, the *meek* who are to inherit the earth (Matt 5:5) and to possess (as sheer gift) the kingdom of heaven (Matt 5:10). "Do not be afraid, little flock," Jesus says in Luke's account of the gospel, "for it is your Father's good pleasure to give you the kingdom" (Luke 12:32).

Such is the kingdom of God, such is the presence and power of God, that burdened with immeasurable grief, we know God's solace, that halting in anguish and despair nigh unto death, we know God's quickening of our spirits through the indwelling in us of his Holy Spirit, that, faulted by conscience or condemned by the verbal assaults of tongues sharpened to speak our shame, we know the unflagging companionship of him of whom it was said—by his enemies, whom he loved—"Look, a glutton and a drunkard [which he was not], a friend of tax collectors and sinners [which he was]" (Matt 11:19b). "Come to me, all you that are weary and carrying heavy burdens," Jesus says, "and you will find rest," divine refreshment, that is what it means, and the happiness of an eternal sabbath (rest for the soul) in the present moment and in the everlasting future. Saint Thomas á Kempis heard and felt Jesus' "Come to me, *all*" and he cried out in prayer:

> Thou art witness unto me, O God, that nothing can comfort me, no creature can give me rest, but Thou only, my God, whom I long to contemplate everlastingly.[10]

"Come to me all . . . All come to me," Jesus says. Christ sets no limit to the blessed all.

And coming, what do we find but that, as Jesus says, "his yoke is easy, and his burden is light." His yoke does not chafe, for it is shaped to our need of it, which is our need of him. And his burden

---

10. See Speer, *Five Minutes a Day*, 276.

is light, for it is the burden of his caring for us as for no one else, and it is the burden of his caring for all others as if for us alone. Centuries ago, Bernard of Clairvaux sang of it in a melody and cadence of victory: "O blessed burden that makes all burdens light! O blessed yoke that bears the bearer up."[11] So also George Frederick Handel in his glorious *Messiah* made it dance in our hearing, so we may sing:

> His yoke is easy
> His burthen is light
> His burthen, his burthen is light![12]

Let Us Pray

O God of Father-Love, of mother-care, press upon us now that blessed burden that makes all burdens light, and fit us with that blessed yoke that bears the bearer up. So may our souls sing and our spirits dance, even in this fleeting moment, sing and dance with that eternal sabbath refreshment promised and kept for us in Jesus Christ, your Son, our Savior and Lord.
Amen.

---

11. See Buttrick, *Interpreter's Bible*, 391.
12. Handel, *Messiah*, 98.

WHAT PEACE WITH GOD BRINGS

A Memorial Day Communion Sermon

Text: Rom 5:1–5

> Since we are justified by faith, we have peace with God through our Lord Jesus Christ, through whom we have obtained access to this grace in which we stand; and we boast in our hope of sharing the glory of God. And not only that, but we also boast in our sufferings, knowing that suffering produces endurance, and endurance produces character, and character produces hope, and hope does not disappoint us, because God's love has been poured into our hearts through the Holy Spirit that has been given to us.

It is all in the past-perfect tense. In other words, it is done, completed, perfected, and it cannot be undone ever, by anything. "Justification: the stable basis for,"[13] not an uncertain goal of life, with faith—*our* faith, timid, and anxious and laced with doubt as it may be—receiving justification, not producing it. And peace with God, deliverance from God's wrath (which is the inevitable consequence of holy love unrequited) given us whose tired hearts may have nearly put to sleep any thought of divine judgment as warranted or even possible. That's the way Calvin saw it.[14] Nevertheless, Christ Jesus stands before us and before God on our behalf. He was made to be sin who knew no sin (2 Cor 5:21). So the word of God in Holy Writ puts it. Then Luther, ever audacious and provocative, echoes the thought: Christ, who never sinned, made for us to be, as it were, the only sinner[15] bearing the sins of the world, as he has "borne our griefs and carried our sorrows" (Isa 53:4 KJV). And he bears and carries them still before his heavenly Father in prayer.

---

13. Hunsinger, "Commentary on Romans," 41.
14. Buttrick, *Interpreter's Bible*, 453.
15. Dillenberger, *Martin Luther*, 134–37.

Further, peace with God through our Lord Jesus Christ brings with it "this grace in which we stand." Grace is a settled condition of divine favor. But more, grace is divine power sufficient to enable us human beings to do the unthinkable: to forgive those who have wronged us not seven times, but seventy-seven times—and more (Matt 18:22). Forgiveness "leaves its arithmetic at home," Lutheran preacher and teacher of preaching Paul Scherer asserted.[16] It can't be calculated. It doesn't add up. Grace also is power to love our enemies, even those enemies determined to maintain their enmity towards us no matter what, and to act on that enmity. At our cynical worst we think it can't be done. Then we see it done—just some short days ago we did—by survivors of a racist slaughter at a prayer meeting at an African Methodist Episcopal Church in the deep south of America the Beautiful. The place: Charleston, South Carolina. The survivors of the slaughter showed up before authorities to confront the perpetrator, but not to condemn the man—the law would take care of that—but to forgive him and to pray for the eternal safety of his soul. Even the press and the politicians were awestruck. What can we say but that those AME Church survivors stood tall in the grace of God given to them through Jesus Christ our Lord? Like "heroes proved in liberating strife," they "loved mercy more than life."[17]

One thing more: the peace we have with God through Jesus Christ our Lord brings with it not only remembrance of justification and this amazing grace in which we stand. It brings with it, as well, an apprehension of divine glory to boast in, or, perhaps better said, to exult in eternally. Exultation in divine glory, as our text attests, is even possible for us in our present moment filled as it is with inglorious deeds, suffering, and seemingly endless terrors. Jesus himself bore up under the weight of such deeds, suffering, and terrors his whole life long, all the way from Bethlehem—think of Herod's slaughter of the innocents—to Jerusalem, which hoped against hope to have nothing to do with Jesus. Plots were hatched in an attempt to get rid of him as quickly and efficiently as possible.

16 Scherer, "A Prayer," 333.

17. Bates, "America the Beautiful," hymn 510.

Jesus bore up under the burden of inglorious deeds, sufferings, and terrors; he carried them as the weight of glory into the courtyard of Caiaphas, all through that notorious show trial before Pontius Pilate, the clamor of an incited mob's vehement demand ringing in his ears: "Crucify him! Crucify him!" (Matt 27:22–23; Mark 15:13; Luke 23:21; John 19:15). The mob, we know, was incited by Jerusalem's religious, and Rome's approved, governing authorities, who had, we might call it, "political smarts." Give them that. "Is it not better," they reasoned, that "one man die" than that the whole of a Roman occupied nation should be brought to ruin (John 11:50)? That *was* the logic of it. And it was logic—cold, calculated, and ruthlessly pursued. In consideration of it, and not in the least diminishing the fearfulness of it, Paul, sometime later, had this to say: take your appointed share in the sufferings of Christ—Paul certainly took his share!—and thereby receive the earnest of everlasting glory, divine glory (Rom 8:17).

In Rom 8:15–17, Paul flings notice of Christ's promised glory right into the heart of our Sunday morning's liturgy of praise, word, prayer, and sacrament. Listen:

> When we cry, [and we do], "Abba! Father!" it is [Christ's] very Spirit bearing witness with our spirit that we are children of God, and, if children, then heirs, heirs of God and joint heirs with Christ—if, in fact, we suffer with him so that we also may be glorified with him. (Rom 8:15–17)

In our prayers, offered with "sighs too deep for words" (Rom 8:26), you can feel the weight of glory as we weep with those who weep and rejoice with those who rejoice (Rom 12:15). More keenly the weight of glory may be felt as with trembling lips we remember, before God, saints of old time and of our own time, martyred, yet, to the very end, believing themselves loved by God and as near to Jesus as their last breath. "Crucified with Christ" (Gal 2:19)! It is the right way to speak of them. And today, this very Lord's day, as martyrs die (women, men, children)—on the evidence we can believe they do—do they hear from Christ Jesus in their faith's alert ear what at least one thief crucified with Christ heard: "Today you will be with me in paradise" (Luke 23:43)?

Christ's glory waits upon our receiving it in faith right here and now at this table so beautifully set in prayer and hope. The bread we break, is it not, by the Spirit, the body of Christ, the bread of life, broken for us? Jesus spoke of it so (John 6:35). And the cup we pour and share, is it not a singular cup, that one dreadful, terrible cup Christ spoke of as his blood "poured out for many" (Mark 14:24) for the forgiveness of sins, the cup of his suffering, and, on account of that, the cup of salvation? "Drink from it, all of you" (Matt 26:27). Please don't think of it as a polite offer. It is the command of our now risen and ascended Lord, a command to be obeyed. Remember what Jesus said to James and John, those aspiring and ambitious sons of Zebedee, when Jesus interrogated them concerning the cup: "Are you able to drink the cup that I drink?" They replied, "We are able." Really? "You will drink of it," Jesus said (Matt 20:22–23; Mark 10:35–40). James and John had no idea what they were getting into. Do we? The late, to my mind great, Princeton theologian, George Stuart Hendry, got it right. He said to PhD students of sacramental theology—so I've been told—"If you could explain it, you wouldn't need it." So without explanation, we obey Christ's command. We eat and we drink in remembrance of Christ's death (that's the theology of the cross, Christ's suffering, his passion) until he comes (that's the theology of glory), never the one without the other. *Christ has died, Christ is risen, Christ will come again!* Christ does come still, his glory hidden in sufferings all around. And he *will* come in *manifest glory*. Until then the psalmist sings of what we are to do now: "O taste and see that the LORD is good" (Ps 34:8)!

Let Us Pray

For your peace that passes understanding, and for all that comes with it: remembrance of justification, grace to sustain us and to cause us to stand, suffering with Christ—however we may be called upon to do so—in anticipation of the glory about to be revealed to us, we praise you O God, in Jesus' name. Amen.

I BELIEVE IN THE CHURCH

Memorial Sunday, May 28, 2022

Text: Matt 28:16–20

> Now the eleven disciples went to Galilee, to the mountain to which Jesus had directed them. When they saw him, they worshiped him; but some doubted. And Jesus came and said to them, "All authority in heaven and on earth has been given to me. Go, therefore, and make disciples of all nations, baptizing them in the name of the Father and of the Son and of the Holy Spirit, and teaching them to obey everything that I have commanded you. And remember, I am with you always, to the end of the age."

"I believe in the holy Catholic Church; the communion of the saints . . ."[18] That is not just my personal confession of faith; it is *our* confession; it is the confession of the Presbyterian Church (USA). It is the confession of the communion of saints worldwide from ancient times to our times, to times beyond our reckoning. That is what catholicity, universality, is all about. The words of our confession, of course, are from the Apostles' Creed, Dr. Undreiner's setting of which was sung by our choir as an offertory anthem. Predating the Apostles' Creed, and the basis for it, is the Nicene Creed, the most ecumenical of all creeds. It states our common confession of faith in these words: "We believe in one holy catholic and apostolic church."[19]

We do not, as a matter of conviction—as opposed to mere opinion—invest our life (which is what belief truly entails) in a building, in a culture, in a political party or ideology. Nor do we invest our life without reserve in a "lifestyle" of our own fashioning. Nor do we throw the whole weight of our life into the preservation of our racial, ethnic, personal, or socioeconomic identity, our celebrated diversity, or our desire to find unity in that diversity. However significant, these are not what theologian Paul Tillich

---

18. *Book of Confessions*, 2.3.

19. *Book of Confessions*, 1.3.

called matters of "ultimate concern."[20] Much less do we believe in, invest our life (lock, stock, and barrel) in, a "my kind of people" kaffeeklatsch of friends made popular decades ago by comedian and late-show television host Jack Paar. Instead, we invest our life in—exercise belief in and through—the church, the communion of saints reaching back into ancient Israel, into first-century Galilee and those earliest doubting and worshiping disciples, and stretching ahead into twenty-first-century doubting, worshiping Ramsey, New Jersey, and beyond.

And in that church, and with those saints, and not apart from them, we invest our life in, we confess our faith in Christ Jesus, crucified, risen, regnant, ascended to the right hand of the Father, who has said to us—we have heard him say it through the witness of the biblical text read this day—"All authority in heaven and on earth has been given to me." It is thoroughly undemocratic. No election by us of Jesus as Lord, but Jesus' election of us to be sainted sinners, his church. More particularly, Jesus' election of you (with your elders, deacons, and pastor) to be his church in this place and time, no matter your wondering, perhaps, what on earth may come of it. This place and these troubling, hard times are yours to make disciples of all people here and now given into your care, baptizing them in the name of the Father and of the Son and of the Holy Spirit, and teaching them (children, adults, confirmation class participants, all) to obey everything that Christ commands, above all his central commandment to love as he loved. And there is no way to have done with that Great Commission, as it is called, but to fulfill it.

"You did not choose me but I chose you" (John 15:16), the apostle John heard Christ Jesus say to his church. And so the word of divine, peremptory election has been continued on to include us. As scholars of the Holy Bible agree, authority in apostolic times and in our time indicates precisely that: the supreme right (the divinely bestowed right) to choose, to appoint to office, to command

---

20. Tillich, *Systematic Theology*, 10, 12–14, 21, 24–25, 28, 36, 42, 50, 53, 110–11, 115, 118, 120–21, 124, 127, 131, 146, 148, 156, 211, 214–16, 218, 220–23, 230, 273.

obedience."[21] Our *being* church, therefore, is not a garment we can don or doff. It is very life to us, life set apart to God in Christ in the power of the Spirit, which is what holiness (or sainthood) is all about. Therefore, we confess "one holy catholic and apostolic church." The church is not ours to make or break. And it certainly is not any preacher's, pastor's, or interim pastor's to save or sink. The church is Christ's to command, just as our life itself is not simply ours to make of it what we will but is Christ's to make of what he will. Jesus never said anything more incessantly, more insistently than this: that those who seek to save their life (to claim it as their own to do with as they please) will lose it, but those who lose their life for his sake and for the sake of the gospel will find it (Matt 16:25; Mark 8:35; Luke 9:24). So also, Paul in faithful echo, "You have died and your life is hidden with Christ in God. When Christ who is your life is revealed then you also will be revealed with him in glory" (Col 3:3–4). Then the eventually martyred Rev. Dr. Martin Luther King Jr., in his address at the 1966 Illinois Wesleyan University convocation said, "If a man has not discovered something that he will die for, in a sense he is not fit to live."[22] Better that a church, any church in any place and time, die for Christ's sake than live for its own sake.

As church, and in the communion of saints, we believe in God the Father Almighty and in Jesus Christ his only Son, Our Lord, and in the Holy Spirit. And with the communion of saints, as Christ's church, we believe in the forgiveness of sins, the resurrection of the body, and the life everlasting. As church our very lives are put at risk, and only so are our lives made secure by him unto whom all authority is given in heaven and on earth. We do not believe the church one, holy, catholic, and apostolic because we believe in ourselves. Instead, as church, in the communion of saints, we believe in, we invest our life in, the Christ who has invested his life in us.

"All authority in heaven and on earth has been given to me," Jesus says. "Go, therefore, and make disciples of all nations,

---

21. Buttrick, *Interpreter's Bible*, 622.

22. King, "Speech," 5.

baptizing them in the name of the Father and of the Son and of the Holy Spirit, and teaching them to obey everything that I have commanded you." Then this, last and not least, "And remember, I am with you always, to the end of the age." We do remember Christ's presence with us at worship, in word and sacrament, prayer and praise, daily in our sometimes anxious thoughts as we seek his presence and guidance, and nightly in the music that sings through our sorrows to mend our wounded hearts. We remember Christ Jesus' investment of his divine life in our human life, his being with us and for us even when we would have none of him. Paul said it with stark clarity: "While we were still weak, at the right time Christ died for the ungodly" (Rom 5:6).

The time was right at Golgotha, the place of the skull; dare we ever forget it? When Christ Jesus, he who already and always was given all authority in heaven and on earth, was crucified. His disciples fled from him, save for his mother and a handful of staunch women. Passersby mocked him: "Save yourself! If you are the Son of God, come down from the cross" (Matt 27:40). Roman power, figuring it had all authority in heaven and on earth, derided him and taunted his kinsman, placarding above his thorn-pierced brow this epithet: "This is Jesus, the king of the Jews" (Matt 27:37), dripping sarcasm, cruel irony. Nevertheless, that bloody scene was God's peremptory strike at principalities and powers promoting terror. And what it was it remains.

I have it on the very best scholarly authority that the Romans—three short decades, or fewer, after Jesus' crucifixion—crucified hundreds in a day on ramps built all along the walls of Jerusalem.[23] And there was God's Christ, himself the vanguard of that martyr host, not taking up the sword to do in his adversaries or calling down legions of angels to save him (as he said he could have done), but dying the victim's death, choosing to do so and loving, forgiving the victimizers. "Love your enemies," he said, and he did. Can we? It makes no earthly sense, only heavenly sense. You could not have imagined it, though Christ himself called it the gospel, the very best of good news, news not of the age at hand but

23. Private conversations with James H. Charlesworth.

the age to come, which he was initiating right there at Golgotha, and before and after, right now. No one could have imagined it: This way, this truth, this life—the only way, truth, life that leads to the Father. Truth's assigned portion, the scaffold, wrong assuming the throne. That's the way nineteenth-century poet, critic, professor, diplomat James Russel Lowell saw it. "Yet that scaffold sways the future," Lowell wrote.[24] And the future includes you and me—if we will have it—here and now, this very day and hour, in this church, in this town, and in towns and cities all around and abroad, from New York to Kyiv, from what's left of Mariupol to what's up in Patterson.

Still people mock the Christ. Still around the globe, hundreds, perhaps thousands, in a single day suffer persecution, even violent death, with him, for that is his promise, to be with them always in everything to the end of the age. No matter you and I may have the trouble believing it, his being with them. The martyrs themselves have believed it to their last breath. So twentieth-century poet-seer William Butler Yeats could speak of them: You can reject an idea out of hand, he acknowledged, but it is harder to dismiss a life. To quote Yeats exactly, "You can refute Hegel but not the saint."[25] The saint, you see, lives the truth. You can make light of Christ. Heaven knows how many do these days! But Christ will not make light of you. As in Scripture, we find: he died for you, he lives for you, he reigns in power for you, he prays for you. And the communion of saints, those who live and who have died in the Lord, in the best of times and the worst, attests his presence with you always (literally all the days, every single one of them) "to the end of the age." We may have our doubts about it. But we also have cause for doubting our doubts. Therefore, we worship, and in our worship, we bear witness to the gospel truth (with the martyrs in the Greek New Testament, the witnesses, often, not always, even unto death). The martyrs signal the end of the age: that is, the end of pretended usurpation of divine rule by secular powers, which means, literally, "powers of the age," states, causes, all manner of governing

24. Lowell, "Once to Every Man," hymn 361.
25. See Hone, *W. B. Yeats*, 510.

17

sovereignties. They are not eternal, but only for the present moment, which age, which fleeting moment, faces its inevitable end in facing Christ. And they are none of them beyond accountability to "the King of kings and the Lord of lords" (Rev 19:16). That accountability includes those sovereignties to which we ourselves have sworn allegiance. When, in the end, the terrorists—God deliver us!—have fled the scenes of devastation they themselves have wrought, when measures of counterterror (such as the arming of Ukraine) at last are no longer needed, when ancient rivalries and hatreds finally have spent all the fuel of their anger and lost their zeal for perpetrating the "wars and rumors of wars" of which we have been warned in holy writ, and when, for the last time, our own "secret infidelities [have seeped] through our cleverest concealments to poison the springs from which other folks must drink,"[26] then we shall know what prophets have known from of old, that "the grass withers, the flower fades, but the word of our God stands forever" (Isa 40:7). Then, too, we shall know that every baptism we have ever witnessed has signaled a cleansing to last an eternity, because, in it, God has attested his own unrelenting love for the infant and the aged, the least and the lost, the soul-soiled and the seemingly Godforsaken, not to mention those unwanted in the here and now.

Then, too, we shall know that all the instruction in Christ's commandments we have provided, however clumsily, has been taken up by God's own Spirit and made to benefit children and women and men in ways we cannot even imagine. Then we shall know that there is no lost good and that there are no hopeless souls, for the soul is God's implanted hope. "God never yet forsook at need the soul that trusted him indeed."[27] So sings the hymn, and so your own soul sings, as does mine, while doubts yet come thronging; but now more as ministering angels to keep our worship poised, centered, not in ourselves but in God, and in God's Christ, who commanded us, who this day commissions us, to remember, to behold (in the Greek), to keep it in view and ever

26. Fosdick, "Forgiveness of Sins," 297.
27. Neumark, "If Thou but Suffer," hymn 344.

in mind, to remember his promise to be with us always, "to the end of the age." I believe in the church. You believe in the church. But here is where our investment of our life in Christ through the church and communion of saints is surely anchored. Christ Jesus himself believes in, invests his own life, in the church, to the end that the church, *this* church, may fulfill Christ's Great Commission to make disciples of all nations, all ethnicities, all races, all persons of all bloods and soils, baptizing them in the name of the Father and of the Son and of the Holy Spirit, and teaching them to obey everything Christ commands. Just so saints are made of sinners and the communion of saints swells in joy to the glory of God. This is Memorial Day Sunday, a Sunday of remembrance. So, Jesus says, "Remember, I am with you always to the end of the age."

Let Us Pray

To you, O God, our God, who by the power at work within us is able to accomplish abundantly far more than all we can ask or imagine, to you be glory in the church, and in Christ Jesus, to all generations, forever and ever. Amen.

THE ANSWER TO OUR GREATEST NEED[28]

Psalms 42–43

"As a deer longs for flowing streams, so my soul longs for you, O God. My soul thirsts for God, for the living God" (Ps 42:1–2a). It is not the prayer of a happy man. It is the prayer of someone who is angry and anxious for cause. He has been banished—who knows why?—to a wild mountain country where the river Jordan takes its rise. Each day he wakes up to the antiphonal crashing of waterfalls, "deep calls to deep at the thunder of your cataracts" (Ps 42:7) and to the taunting of oppressors, a taunting he cannot get out of his mind: "Where is your God?" (Ps 42:3b).

Echoes of the psalmist's lament can be heard in the cries of children dunned with abusive language, pestered, bullied, mocked: "Sticks and stones may break my bones but words will never hurt me." It is more plea than assertion. It is said to keep from crying. What comes to mind, from some decades back, is the young California AIDS victim and his family, harassed out of town by their neighbors. Where was their God? Then, too, there may be the memory of that cruel moment when our own need of God was ridiculed by someone who felt no such need. So the need grew stronger, more insistent, even desperate; and it seemed no passage of Scripture, no sermon, no prayer, no hymn, no anthem, no requiem mass could meet it. On his deathbed, Rudyard Kipling was asked by his nurse, "Is there anything you need?" The poet and spinner of tales replied, "I need God."[29] The psalmist, therefore, prays not only for himself, but for us all: "My soul thirsts for God, for the living God" (Ps 42:2a).

The need of God is not brought on by dire circumstance. It is brought on by the vivid remembrance of what it is like to truly live and to praise God. "These things I remember, as I pour out my soul: how I went with the throng, and led them in procession to the house of God, with glad shouts and songs of thanksgiving, a

---

28. Originally published in Bartow, *God's Human Speech*, 164–69.

29. Campbell, *Grit to Grapple*, 150.

multitude keeping festival" (Ps 42:4). But what if the pain becomes so severe that there is barely a memory of anything, including worship? What if the pain itself is nearly all there is, hour after hour, day after day, year in and year out? Anna Akhmatova, in her poem "Requiem," suggests what such pain must be like. She says of the Stalinist years in the former Soviet Union that they were "a time when only the dead smiled, happy in their peace,"[30] delivered from their wars.

Not all wars are waged across such vast terrain. Some are waged within the confines of a single soul. "Do not go gentle into that good night," Dylan Thomas cried out as it were, at his father's bier; "rage, rage against the dying of the light."[31] Our psalmist rages, "Vindicate me, O God, and defend my cause against an ungodly people; from those who are deceitful and unjust deliver me!" (Ps 43:1). He does not bear his pain in stoic silence. He storms his way through it with tears and prayers, his jaw set, his fists clenched, maybe.

Rage can have its reasons. When euphemisms such as "ethnic cleansing" are used—as they were by Serbian forces clearing Muslim Croats out of their own cities—it is time for loud lamentation, isn't it? Who will not lament attempts to enlist the one true God as a tribal deity to bless this or that clan or race or class or cause or nation? Closer to home, when someone you know hits rock bottom in a world that seems too often indifferent to its failures and to its poorest and weakest and loneliest, and when even God seems not to care, "Why have you cast me off?" (Ps 43:2a) some poor soul shouts. Then it is time to take up the prayer of the psalmist, isn't that so? Then it is time to hurl some thunder of your own toward heaven.

No sad psalmist ever was meant to pray alone. Instead, the people of God were given the responsibility to pray with him and to take up his prayer for him if at last his voice gave out. So we have in our Bible a psalter full of lamentation, an ancient hymnody to

---

30. Akhmatova, "Requiem 1935–1940," 128.
31. Thomas, "Do Not Go Gentle," 128.

remind us of our need of God, and the solidarity we have with all who share that need.

It is hard not to want to praise God when once you have known what that praise is all about. Therefore, our psalmist sings out of the thick of his troubles: "By day the Lord commands his steadfast love and at night his song is with me, a prayer to the God of my life" (Ps 42:8). He can no more quiet that song of praise than he can silence the taunting of his oppressors or stop his own tears. It is with him. It surrounds him. It has hold of him. It will not let him go. His wounded body aches with the singing of it. Harassed and injured people across millennia have known that ache: African Americans, once purchased for slavery, then singing, praying their way toward freedom or death, they never knew which—"Nobody knows the trouble I've seen, nobody knows but Jesus, nobody knows the trouble I've seen. Glory! Hallelujah!"[32] Lamentation is not the opposite of praise to God. It is what needs to be done in order to praise God "when life tumbles in."[33] Hear the psalmist again: "Why are you cast down, O my soul, and why are you disquieted within me? Hope in God; for I shall again praise him, my help and my God" (Ps 42:5–6, 11; 43:5).

In singing his song, the psalmist is not begging special favors from God. He is not asking for a way through life henceforth cleared of anything that could bruise him. "The thousand natural shocks that flesh is heir to"[34] have been shocks to him no less than to anybody else; and they will be. Beyond that, to paraphrase Langston Hughes, "life for [him] ain't been no crystal stair."[35] The vindication he seeks and the deliverance from oppressors he has every right to demand are not sought as ends in themselves. The psalmist wants vindication and deliverance so that he once again can praise God free of restraint: "O send out your light and your truth; let them lead me; let them bring me to your holy hill and to your dwelling. Then I will go to the altar of God, to God my

32. "Nobody Knows the Trouble I've Seen."
33. Gossip, "When Life Tumbles In," 198.
34. Shakespeare, *Hamlet*, act 3, sc. 1, ll. 62–62.
35. Hughes, "Mother to Son," 67.

exceeding joy; and I will praise you with the harp, O God, my God" (Ps 43:3–4).

When you have sung the majestic and humorous, romantic and antic, thoroughly human and nearly divine music of Haydn's *Creation*—a work Robert Shaw once called an achievement of genius that comes once in a millennium—you could not be blamed for hoping to get over a case of laryngitis so that you could sing it again. When you have burst into tears at the subtle beauty of a delicate Renoir gown rustling across a canvas, you could not be faulted for hoping to see it again and again and again. And the prose of Flannery O'Connor, and the poetry of Elizabeth Barrett Browning:

> How do I love thee? Let me count the ways.
> I love thee to the depth and breadth and height
> My soul can reach, when feeling out of sight
> For the ends of Being and ideal grace.[36]

Does anyone really think the world would be richer if no one ever read such works—or the Bible that inspired them?

Above all, what of the lives you and I have known, the flawed loves that have made us what we are, for better or worse? Is there no remembrance of any of them worth clinging to? Have we no hope for them beyond their return to dust? The Shorter Catechism asserts that humanity's chief end is to glorify God and to enjoy God forever.[37] Human need of God, therefore, is not a sign of weakness; it is a sign of strength. It is our reason for being. No need of Haydn? No need of Renoir? No need of Flannery O'Connor? No need of Elizabeth Barrett Browning? No need of Scripture? No need of you, or of me, or of those who have loved us—or tried to— often beyond their strength? No need of God? The mind boggles. More than anything, more than life as we know it, we need God; and we needn't be ashamed of that. It is the measure of our stature as human beings. "As a deer longs for flowing streams, so my soul longs for you, O God. My soul thirsts for God, for the living God" (Ps 42:1–2a).

---

36. Barrett Browning, "How Do I Love Thee!" 349.

37. *Book of Confessions*, 7.001.

But what of the living God? Is there any evidence that God cares that we need him? When people cry to God, does God hear? When they sing and shout their praise, does it matter at all? As for the psalmist, we haven't the slightest clue whether or how his specific requests were answered. Perhaps he was vindicated. Perhaps he was delivered from "those who are deceitful and unjust" (Ps 43:1b). Perhaps, at last, he did get back to Jerusalem, to the temple, to the altar of God, his "exceeding joy" (Ps 43:4). Or perhaps just as likely—perhaps more likely—he was left in the wilderness with his hopes and his prayers and his pain until the end of his days. That could have happened. It has happened often enough. And if, in fact, that is what happened, would we have to conclude that the psalmist got no answer from God, that God was deaf to him, indifferent to him, or—worse yet—powerless to do anything for him? Some would say so. Others, however, including our psalmist, would not say so; for they know that vindication and deliverance and Jerusalem and the temple and the altar are not answers to prayer in any worthwhile sense of the term if they are themselves godless. If the soul truly "thirsts for God, for the living God" (Ps 42:2), only God will do.

Therefore, we pray to God to bear our reproach with us and for us if we cannot simply be rid of it. And we cannot simply be rid of it. We can pray to God to see us through the valley of the shadow if there is no way around it. And, at last, there is no way around it for anybody. We pray to God to fill our prayers with the breath, with his own Spirit, to give voice to our lament, as to our praise, when our voices give out. And God does: on the lips of Jesus—Ps 22, from the cross, another prayer of lament on its way to praise— "My God, my God why have you forsaken me?" (Ps 22:1). We pray to God to fill our mortal flesh with divine glory, until the tears that have been our food day and night (Ps 42:3) turn to Eucharist and song. When the soul "thirsts for God, for the living God" (Ps 42:2), God will answer. God will give himself to us as already he has given himself to us, in an agony of bliss, of heavenly joy.

> Why are you cast down, O my soul,
> And why are you disquieted within me?

Hope in God; for I shall again praise him,
My help and my God. (Ps 45:5)

Let Us Pray

We turn to you in our need O God, glad to know that already you have provided for it. We thank you for the psalmist who has voiced our need so well and for the Christ who has met our need so fully. Keep us ever alert to your presence, vouchsafed to us in Christ in the best of times and in the worst, that we may have courage to pray without ceasing and to live in hope. Amen.

CHAPTER TWO

New and Selected Poems
of Charles L. Bartow

Introductory Essay to Chapters 2 and 3

ELIZABETH BARRETT BROWNING, A devout nineteenth-century poet whose works are read with appreciation and profit to this day, aimed at something higher than the use of language to spin out startling images and fancies of human invention free of the constraints of truth-telling in relation to life and living persons. Her witness to life was not only poetic; it was theopoetic. In "The Dead Pan" she makes it clear that she sought inspiration not from the mythic muse, but from God, the God and the Father of her Lord—and ours—Jesus Christ. In just a few lines from the thirty-ninth stanza, Barrett Browning sets the mark for herself and other poets of serious intent:

> Truth is fair: should we forgo it?
> Can we sigh right for a wrong?
> God himself is the best Poet,
> And the Real is his song.
> Sing his truth out fair and full,
> And secure his beautiful.
> Let Pan be dead![1]

---

1. Barrett Browning, "Dead Pan," 191.

My brother, Ernie, and I—I dare to speak for both of us—do not aim to bear false witness in our poems to others' lives or to our own. Instead, our aim is to tell the truth at least as far as we can see it and tell it from where we stand. And certainly we do not stand above the crowd. We are embedded in a compromised human situation. We are as theologians say *simul justus et peccator*, at once justified and sinful. In his commentary on Galatians, Luther wrote,

> A Christian . . . is both righteous and a sinner, holy and profane, an enemy of God and yet a child of God.[2]

I believe that Ernie and I also aim to let our poems, themselves, live *their* truth. The poems certainly are not independent of us, for we have written them. Nevertheless, we find them strangely resistant to our subscription of them into the exclusive service of our own will and purpose, even when composed in the first person. I think the great twentieth-century poet Robert Frost had something like that in mind when he asserted that a poem "cannot be worried into existence."[3] Presbyterian theologian H. H. Farmer and others observed that human history is a history of persons in relationship to God and to each other.[4] In other words, none of us is independent of one another any more than a poem's life is independent of its maker. The life of a poem is virtual, not actual. Yet it is a virtual life that is something very different from the mere self-expression of the poet. In her celebrated theory of art titled *Feeling and Form*, Susanne K. Langer stated the matter this way:

> The poet's business is to create the appearance of 'experiences', the semblance of events lived and felt, and to organize them so they constitute a purely and completely experienced reality, a piece of virtual life.[5]

I do not know if Ernie and I have succeeded in our attempts at poetry that witnesses to lived truth. That is for others to decide.

2. Dillenberger, *Martin Luther*, 130.
3. Frost, "The Figure a Poem Makes," 49.
4. Hinderliter, "Biblical Interpretation," 22.
5. Langer, *Feeling and Form*, 212.

But as preaching is an attempt at faithful witness to life in Christ and to life as people actually live it so too poetry is meant to tell the truth. Poetry and preaching are distinct forms of witness. Nevertheless, both, to put it in contemporary colloquial terms, try to "tell it as it is."

The poems in chapter 2 are new and selected poems by me, Charles (Chuck) Louis Bartow. The poems are arranged under the following headings: Life on Holy Days and Holidays, Lives Gone and Going By, Late Life Reflections, and Lived Moments with Nature.

Chapter 3 is a collection of poems composed by my brother, Ernest Winfield Bartow. Ernie's poems, all in free verse, seem to me at once pastoral and prophetic, personal, and, at times, autobiographical. I am happy and privileged (with Ernie's permission) to include them in this volume. Though often publicly performed in various venues, none have been published in print until now. My brother's essay on William Stringfellow (adapted from his ThM thesis at Princeton Theological Seminary) is taken from a diary he is keeping especially for his children, grandchildren, and great-grandchildren. Decades ago Ernie's thesis "William Stringfellow, Model of a Resurrectional Perceptual Field" was published in the *Indiana Speech Journal*.

Life on Holy Days and Holidays

Christmas Eve Psalms, 2018
See 1 Kgs 19:12, KJV, NRSV.
Also see Luke 2:14; Rev 2:28

Lamentation

This Christmas Eve is dumb, no angels sing;
All heaven's quiet as a tomb tonight.
It is a Christmas Eve of darkness, fright,
A mournful eve wherein sad souls must fling
Their wearied hopes into a failing spring
Of love, of kindness, goodness. Oh! The sight
Brings an alarm. Shall wrong prevail, not right?

Praise

A still small voice, a sound of sheer silence;
above earth's din, for those with ears to hear,
the heav'nly host cries out, "Glory to God!"
and herald angels sing of peace on earth,
while, in the east, the *morning star* appears
brightening westward through the deep of night.
Amidst uncomprehending darkness—light!

Bourne to Birth

Mary's Call to Bear the Word

(Luke 1:26–38, cf. Isa 6:8b)

She was a prophet bold and yet afraid
  since she was favored to carry the Word,
    not on her lips alone, but in her womb,
      blest servant of the Servant Word she bore,
The Mother of the Son of the Most High,
  Jesus, Savior, God's lowly human form
    Spirit conceived in Mary's virgin flesh,
      Mary, who said, "Here am I, let it be. . . ."
How can it be that "The Mother of God"[6]
  should be as plain a maid as Yeats described,
    and promised bride of Joseph, an obscure
      tradesman, a carpenter from Galilee
That Gentile nowheresville in Palestine?
  And how can I in my own far off place,
    two thousands years and more removed from her
      and her pregnancy's strange coming to be,
Care, as I do, to know the Word she bore
  as Ever-living Word my saving truth?
    The search for certitude cannot avail
      except faith birth the Word she bore in me.

TO MARY

Crèche Reflections and Christmas Greetings, 2019

Dear Mary: word's come down the infant's yours
Swaddled and lying there in manger straw,
Your boy-child, Son of Providence as well,
Though many disbelieve it in our time.
No matter, rest yourself, quiet your thoughts.
Let Joseph standing by, keep watch and ward.

6. Yeats, "Mother of God," 248.

Quite soon enough you'll ponder your child's fate
At tyrant hands, the slaughtered innocents,
The hurried flight to where your ancients fled
Foreshadowing the passion, cross, and grave
And victory your child at last would win
For you, for us, despotic pow'r dethroned
By love, holy, divine, stronger than death,
Incarnate, mothered, cradled in your care.

A CHRISTMAS PRAYER, AD 2020

Uttered in light of the springtime attack of the COVID-19
pandemic.

Midwinter's bleak with memories of spring
When all the gushing viruses of fear
Despair, and death's dreadful imaginings
Made sun-warmed flesh feel cold as living stone.
Sequestered, worried souls shivered alone
And waited out what was declared a war
Against an unseen foe. And still souls wait,
Yet not without an anxious hope the tide
Of war may turn, the grim foe be restrained
At last, perhaps destroyed. Let it be so!
O God, let it be so! Let Christmas come
As first it came in dark, cold climes of fear
With threat of death unleashed by viral powers:
Let Christ be born in unsequestered souls.

A QUESTION OF HEARING

Christmastide 2021

Strong winds are whistling through the Norway spruce
Its green all wintered white in fresh wet snow.
The whistling can be heard as nature's call
To Saturnalian raucous revelry,

Or given ears to hear it, Spirit-speech,
Hymned summons to attend the Word made flesh,
In poet song, a call to holy joy:
"Light for the path of life and God brought near."[7]
This Christmastide will those with ears to hear
—HEAR—
And whistle on strong winds joy to the world?

OUT OF WOMAN

"Then the man said, 'This at last is bone of my bones and flesh of my flesh; this one shall be called Woman, for out of Man this one was taken.'" (Gen 2:23)

". . . the Lord has created a new thing on the earth: a woman encompasses a man." (Jer 31:22)

"Blessed are you among women, and blessed is the fruit of your womb." (Luke 1:42)

". . . conceived by the Holy Ghost, born of the virgin Mary . . ." (The Apostles' Creed)

The angel Gabriel, God-sent, we're told,
Arrived at the virginal door, entered
With a knock of promise, and left Spirit,
Seminal life, to nurture infant flesh
In maiden bliss, vibrant, hospitable.
"Let it be with me," she'd said, no reserve,
"According to your word." And that was that.
The Spirit-flesh grew, announced readiness
To be born, to suffer. Her suffering,
Love's labor, brought to rude nativity
The angel-promised Child, the Son of God
And blessed Mary's boy, her very own,
Bone of her bone, flesh of her flesh alone.
Out of Woman, the "Man of sorrows" grown.

7. Knapp, "Lord God of Hosts," hymn 432.

NATIVITY'S VERDICT

(Matt 2:1–8, Luke 2:8–20)

A stable-cry shatters the onyx sky
Into myriad crystals ringing joy,
Singing hope through the Herodian dark.
Coarse men, swarthy, stinking of sheep and sweat,
Start at the sound and sight, get word of peace,
Run as instructed to the rude manger
Where angel-dreams cradle heaven's tidings
To safety from tyranny's child-vexed weal.
The shepherds tell it all. All are amazed
At what they tell, not least we who ponder
With mother Mary the disquieting
Events of this night—the shattering cry,
The ringing, singing, news-filled onyx sky:
No peace for those with whom God is not pleased?

DOXOLOGY

An Advent-Christmas Commemorative Recollection

Advent-Christmas came and went
Charged with good news heaven-sent:
Triumph o'er the *saeculum*
By the *lasting* age to come,
Human beings out of thrawl
To the evils that appall,
Hatreds, fears no longer fed,
Wars, rumors of wars found dead
With the advent of God's Christ,
Son of God, true Light of Light,
All dark time-being-sadness
Bright with God's promised gladness;
The turning of the ages
Foretold by Israel's sages,

The End made the Beginning
With hallelujahs ringing!

EPIPHANY IN DECLINE

(Sunday morning, 8:45 am)

Fall comes on now with all its promised bite,
Dawn's frost, evening's dank breath, noon's failing warmth.
Spirit's ample flesh thins soon to feel cold
Winter's burning blast of white-out weather.
The blinding clarity of freezing air
Alerts the mind to what's in store for it:
Sluggishness, some last thoughts icing over,
Summer unremembered, spring longer gone,
The past a grave for every once bright hope,
The heavy earth falling. Yet there's a sense
Of life not only behind and before
This autumn onset of the end of things,
But here, now, in the thick of dying days.
Hear choirs singing, preachers bravely preaching
That Living Word, the way, the truth, the life
For seasons coming on, forgotten, all!

THE MOURNING AFTER EASTER

There is a leafless tree
That bore upon its limbs
The figure of a man
Heard breathing his last breath,
A sound of sheer silence.
And in that silent sound,
Disquieting good news:
Listen! *Crucifixus*
Etsiam pro nobis.
Is this the tree of life?

A NEW YEAR'S EVE PAUSE

No "fah lah lah lah lah, lah lah lah lah,"
No Deck the Halls, no singing "auld lang syne,"
No toasting the old year now soon gone by,
No hailing the new year so close at hand,
The hall, undecked, falls quiet as a morgue.
Alone, attentive in this silent space
Where unsung goings out and comings in
Have the feel of prayers not worth the candle,
I wonder what this passing's all about:
The failures of the year that's ending here,
The prospect of more failing years to come?
Do I detect the ending of an age,
Await my old self's soundless dying off?
Or could this be the pause wherein God speaks
Creatio ex nihilo again?

MEMORIAL DAY THOUGHTS

28 May, 2018

In ancient Israel tidings
  of good news to the poor gave kings
    legitimacy for their reign
      in Yahweh's feared and holy name.

From Macedonia and Greece
  to Rome the conquerors' shout was "Peace!"
    long sought, vouchsafed prosperity
      For yielding subjects bound, yet free.

From colonial empires vast
  the common good of all was cast
    as warrant for enforced demands
      to governance of distant lands.

Now in our patriot dreams we hear:
  "Democracy, freedom from fear

and want, at home, abroad attained,
    must be secured, by might maintained!"

This summons clear—what soul can doubt?—
    is what the state must be about.
      Yet this just cause holds at its core
        the brutal industry of war.

IN TIME OF WAR: A REMINDER

As the 2022 invasion of Ukraine continues

"We will all stand before the judgment seat of God." (Rom 14:10)

Still today the minions
Of the Satanic host
Spread their blood-stained pinions
East to west, coast to coast.
Wars and rumors of wars–
Wars yet to come—abound.
Our ancient myths hold Mars
Still leads his forces round.
But though moderns agree
Myth's god of war is dead,
What *is* alive we see
Is human vaunt instead.
Unbridled nation states
With Satanic powers,
Full armored with their lusts
Piled and piled in towers
Of might that makes their right
Hegemony, an end
Held clearly in full sight,
All lesser powers left
As best they can to fend
For themselves, quite bereft
Of what's required clearly
For hope of victory.

Yet, "Oh! Say can you see"
Victory still loom
Midst the horrific gloom?
Tried faith will not forget
God is the ruler yet:
The victors, vanquished meet
Before God's judgment seat.

Late Life Reflections

PSALM 90:10, 12, 17 (KJV)
A Prayer of Moses, the man of God.

The days of our years are threescore years and ten;
and if by reason of strength they be fourscore years,
yet is their strength labor and sorrow;
for it is soon cut off and we fly away.
So teach us to number our days,
that we may apply our hearts unto wisdom.
And let the beauty of the Lord our God be upon us:
And establish thou the work of our hands upon us;
yea, the work of our hands establish thou it.

NUMBERING MY DAYS

A Late-Life Pondering of Ps 90:10, 12, 17

My life's a life of unremembered dreams,
Dreams doubtless worth the unremembering.
But glad and nightmare scenes from yesteryears,
Like vagrants sheltered in a run-down house,
Still haunt my mind and stir up hopes and fears
And thoughts of all that's been and yet may be.
I ask myself while numbering my days
As I approach my fourscore years and ten,
Mortality in view, this reckoning,

What will it yield for me? What Moses prayed:
A heart of wisdom kept in steadfast love,
My handiwork God blest, God's beauty seen,
Inheritance of weal and not of woe?
My life cut off, I'll fly away; I'll know?

NOCTURNAL REVERIE

In quiet night, before the dawn struck light
Across the Hudson, eastward of our town,
I lay awake, quite silent as the night,
And listened for what thoughts I might bring down
From off the shelves of memory's tiered height:
Perhaps some mirthful moments, joys, to crown
An evening's playful fancies with delight;
Or—more likely?—perplexities, a brown
Study, deep and melancholic, to blight
My nighttime reverie, steal joy, and drown
Nocturnal hope of glad recall, give fright
To what the dawn might bring. A feckless clown
Am I, to think, to hope, try as I might,
To wear, come dawn, a smile and not a frown.

NOCTURNAL GIFTS

It's the dreaming that makes the night worthwhile,
the happy and the nightmare dreams alike,
strange and macabre virtualities
that make the actualities of day
less than the ALL they ever seem to be:

Distressing fear of loss of faith, hope, love,
diminishment of soul to sense of self,
the physical decline all bodies know,
the faculties of mind that face decay
earth's warming unto death as is alleged.

39

O Blessed night, O respite from regret
 and from the anxious thoughts of wakeful hours,
  you're rightly honored for the gifts you bring,
   unsought, unmerited, gladly received
    as pleasant dreams, and nightmare scenes, and *Life*!

AN OCTOGENARIAN'S LAMENT

"A time to keep silence," Eccl 3:7

Eight decades into life its come to this:
A time for silence, to refrain from speech.
I hold my tongue at what I see around:
The triumph of Baalistic anarchy,
Illimitable license for the self
To fashion for itself a self set free
From any moral claim outside itself.
There are no "unclean and forbidden ways"[8]
The mind can wander into now it seems.
My reservations—silenced!—are so quaint
As to be scorned, and they are roundly scorned
As retrograde concerns rightly condemned.
How long, O Lord, how long! Must I endure
This silencing, this scorn, to my last breath?

STRANGE VISIONINGS

The old man's bedtime visionings were strange.
 His dimmed eyes closed, he still saw faces clear,
  Some unfamiliar, some publicly well-known,
   Like photographic images of lives
    That mattered to him somehow, who knows why?
     Or should have mattered? Oh yes, there's the rub.
      What lives should not have mattered one might ask;
       Aborted lives of children in the womb,

8. Baillie, *Diary of Private Prayer*, 49.

Or lives of newborn babies dead at birth,
Soon buried, lives of little consequence:
The bodily and mentally impaired
Who, at their best, grunt happiness or rage?
Who has not seen and treasured every one?
Strange visionings at bedtime tell it all.

A WEARIED WITNESS

". . . since it is by God's mercy that we
are engaged in this ministry
we do not lose heart." (2 Cor 4:1)

The old preacher
totters his way
to the pulpit,
His posture stooped,
his prayerful soul
heavy with years.

Yet still he hopes
somehow to turn
ink into blood,
Let God be God
in halting speech:
the Word made flesh,

Full
of Grace
and Truth.

BEFORE THE END OF TIME

"Do not cast me off in the time of
old age;
do not forsake me when my
strength is spent." (Ps 7:9)

Some time before the end of time he sits,
  an old man sipping bourbon and tonic
    he sits, quite spent, bereft even of thought,
      feeling loss of what he'd long hoped to be:

A Christian gentleman, virtuous, wise,
  always in pursuit of "the right, the good,
    and the happy," proving himself neighbor[9]
      to the neighborless wounded, poor, afraid.

But now, no strength left for high ambition,
  glad aspiration's moment come and gone,
    worn-out before the end of time, he waits,
      helpless to know what at time's end he'll be.

TONIGHT NO EVENING STAR

Psalm 139:11–12

Tonight no evening star, no moon to pierce
The steep descent of overspreading night
Or keep night's near and haunting death owl still,
Or quiet thoughts of conscience stirred to life
From out the darkened past, thoughts, memory,
Unbridled, brings to present consciousness:
The cruelty of subtly crafted slights,
The smiles, oft' smiled, to hide the heart's cold sneer,
Mean jokes, well told, at some poor soul's expense
For laughter from the sycophantic crowd—
Stern thoughts that drive the conscience-stricken self
At last to cringe at what's done and said.
Disquieting the death-hoots of the owl
That haunt the starless, moonless night's descent,
Yet blessed still the dark that brings to light
What memory must cause the self to see
Since, darkened, it's not seen itself aright.

9. Ramm, *Right*, 50.

SONNET ON A SOUL'S DESCENT

My soul when young would dance across the sky,
And sing among the Pleiades a song
So sweet, so bright, the stars all sang along.
A canticle of praise to God on high.
The planets with their moons joined in to cry
Their hallelujahs, a cherubic throng
To overwhelm and silence every wrong
Of earth's deep night, and quiet every lie.
But then the sisters' griefs became my own.
Through galaxies of loss my soul plunged down
To halt among sad Sheol's shadowed forms.
My canticle of praise became a groan
The heavenly hallelujahs could not drown,
And deep earth's furies shrieked through skyless storms.

Lives Gone By and Going By

DORIS

I don't know why she came to mind just now,
But there she is and so I'll speak of her:
Her face a wrinkled caramel of mirth
Her crown, all white, announcing she was sage
And so she was, a wise and caring soul,
A person you could turn to in distress.
She prayed to God as to a trusted friend,
And hearing her you'd sense that God was there
A Presence inexplicable yet felt
As surely as the breath it takes to pray,
Her voice, Jamaican gladness, rhythmic joy.
Like "all the saints who from their labors rest,"
She's held in memory and treasured there,
And never mind the world at large can't care.

NAMES EVER KEPT

"Whose names are in the book of life." (Phil 4:3)

They said no one would miss her when she died,
None mourn her passing. Who "they" are, who knows?
But one suspects the "they" are merely one,
Or few, or several who saw her life
As something to despise, her drunkenness

And drug-addicted days, all long ago,
A judgment everlasting, so to say,
A warrant to dismiss her last, hard days
Of pain, and prayer, sobriety, and praise
As insufficient recompense for sin,
Not sin against the God whom she adored,
But sin against their standard of success
Defined as wealth or some accomplishment
That's worth at least a measure of acclaim.
Her mediocrity's what gave offense,
Though mediocre, from the Latin, means
"Halfway up the rugged mountain." Not bad!
Names such as hers, whom they'd have us forget,
Are written in "the book of life," there kept.
This I believe and so herewith attest.

THE CHOICE

Before he'd died he'd given up on God,
Would praise God, preach, and pray, and sing no more.
It was horrendous evil wrecked his faith,
Or so he said. I take him at his word
For who am I to judge veracity,
Though often it is true we're self-deceived
In things that matter most, like life and death
And doing good or harm, or dodging both
So doing nothing bold or tentative
To make the slightest difference where we live.
He said he was agnostic, just not sure
That there can be a God of steadfast love
If the created order that God's made
Seems everywhere a sacrifice of life
To violence, to suffering, to pain
Enduring, everlastingly acute.
And so he'd planned assisted suicide,
A legal and a merciful way out

Of all that troubled his agnostic mind.
Some may not ever think his choice was wise,
But it was his, and no more's to be said.
He was my friend, so I'm disquieted
That doubts that trouble faith can be so strong.

THE DANDELION LADY

"... do not worry, saying 'What will we eat?' or 'What will we
drink?'" (Matt 6:31)

Her garb was shapeless, ankle length, and black,
   and stooped, alert, she searched the wild grass field
      across the street from where we children watched.
         We wondered who she was—or what—a witch?

Our young minds traveled on along that way.
   From time to time she stopped, reached down, and picked
      what we were taught to pluck up, throw away,
         those dandelions ruinous to lawns.

She went on searching, picking quite some time
   and placed all she picked in a burlap sack,
      then turned to leave. We quit our watchful post
         still thinking her quite weird if not a witch.

Some twenty years and more gone by, I came
   to know what she was up to in that field.
      From dandelion leaves, salads are made
         and from their blossoms, dandelion wine.

No witch's brew that sweet intoxicant,
   but rather, on a weekday afternoon,
      a welcomed respite from late midweek chores.
         All praise for dandelions green and gold!

And praise for the bent lady in that field
   long ago, awake to nature's bounty,
      divine provision for the poor. Praise God
         for dandelion salad and good wine.

PRAISE

Most often they come just after sunrise,
   young men, muscular, lithe, quick, balletic,
      leaping off the rear ends of massive trucks,
      darting to opposing curbs, dungareed

Gene Kellys somehow avoiding the threat
   posed by rear-coming, oncoming traffic,
      the morning hour's frantic commutation,
      to hoist the refuse of our careless lives

As if it were their joy, this cleaning up
   of leftovers from our polite tables.
      Garbage men and recycling collectors
      making the streets we live on clear of waste.

Not mentioned in our celebrated books
   of poetry and prose—nor in our prayers?—
      nor lauded by famed critics in *The Times*,
      their sunrise choreography shouts, "Praise!"

BASSAMAT AL-FARAH

(The Smile of Joy)

A sonnet composed following the terrorist destruction of the World Trade Center Towers in New York City, and related atrocities of September 11, 2001. The smile of joy on the lips of the suicide bombers indicates their belief that their death is a martyr's death. Such a death is their guarantee of entrance into paradise.

Last night my mother came to me in dreams
To tuck me in and help me say my prayers,
As long ago she used to climb the stairs
To where I'd lie awake, in dread of schemes
Drawn up by attic demons who, with screams
Of terror, hauled young children to their lairs
And turned them into demons with no cares—

No souls for caring. Mother's prayers cast beams
Of searing light against the nightmare dark,
And still they do, as I attempt to pray
My rage at careless demons in the sky
Bassamat al-farah etched cold and stark
Upon their lips, who crash in flame and flay
Grown children's souls for whom fierce mothers cry.

Lived Moments with Nature

A LATE VERNAL MOMENT OBSERVED

Five o'clock am
   the late spring air
      fifty-two degrees fahrenheit.

Looking east:
   at the horizon,
      low over the Palisades,

A white gold cradle moon
   to rock awake
      the sleeping dawn.

SPRING'S BEGINNING

Spring's beginning—
   ten inches of
      winter white
         flakes like blossoms

falling wet, heaped high
   heavy on roofs
      tree limbs, trucks, cars,
         power lines, cables,

blanketing frozen earth's

greens, sidewalks, roadways,
   hooded pedestrians,
      shoulders hunched,

a shivering beauty—
   calls to mind
      Holy Writ's ancient warning:
         the Devil's descending,

a seeming angel
   of light, of white?
      Spring's beginning,
         when it ends

will leave us
   what
      to sing of
         or to dread?

HAPPINESS BANISHED

An Agitated Interrogative

Just now saw a long-beaked, great-tailed grackle
Peck to death a sparrow in our birdbath.
Startled, appalled at such brutality,
Instinctually instanced, I should guess,
Not planned like acts of human violence,
Banished my early morning happiness,
Replaced it with disquiet, the dark thought
That from the start, perhaps, this fault was there
In all that's been created and called good—
By God. Is that the case? Calvin thought not.
Instead he said a falling out with God,
Our human will to act God's part ourselves,
Imparted on the heavens, on the earth
And all earth's creatures, a condemnation
That only God's restoring grace at work

In us could rectify. That may be true.
But till the rectifying deed is done,
Completed in us, in creation whole,
I'll stay appalled the once called "noble bird,"
The grackle, pretending to the raptor's
Part, killed that bathing sparrow, not for food,
As raptors kill to live, but what, for sport?

Comment
"The condemnation of [humankind] is imprinted on the heavens, and on the earth and all creatures. It hence also appears to what excelling glory the [sons and daughters] of God shall be exalted; for all creatures shall be renewed in order to amplify it and render it illustrious."
John Calvin on Rom 8:19–21[10]

AVIARY SPLENDOR

The goldfinch at the thistle feeder dines,
His yellow gold a treasure all his own.
When he departs, the purple finch arrives
And perches as a monarch on his throne.
Diminutive in stature, he surveys
His vast domain of peace and songbird praise.
This aviary splendor brings to mind
The holiness of beauty, how it's worth
Cannot be calculated in such sums
As human minds can track. The beautiful
Is infinite, deep as eternity,
Is amplified throughout all space and time.
Though tiny as a gold or purple finch
This beautiful commands a cosmic joy.

10. Bartow, "Commentary on Romans," 84.

Comment: God is beautiful (see Ps 27:4) and all true beauty reflects the beauty of divine truth and the relationship of creation to the Creator as distance.[11]

PREVAILING BREEZES

There are breezes
but they're hot
no slightest refreshment
in them.
They are out of the west
where I once lived
and felt hot breezes
nine months ev'ry year.
I'm not complaining here
just taking note:
weather, west to east,
will have its way
and never mind
what easterners prefer.
Prevailing breezes, hot,
blow west to east.

RED PLANET REFLECTIONS

October 8th 2020 and Following

Right now tonight and every night this month
Clear on until the breaking of the dawn,
The planet Mars glows in the eastern sky,
A spangled glory brighter than the stars,
Fair Venus (evening, morning star) outshone.
The moon itself is rivaled. Mars draws near
To earth, red planet thought the god of war
In ancient Rome's heroic, mythic world.

11. See Hart, *Beauty of the Infinite*, 18.

But we have long since quit the mythic scene.
We sense today that war is earthbound strife,
Is human wrought, is waged for human ends
Considered worthy, righteous, warranted,
Necessitating bloody means: godlike
Imaginations of the human heart.

A QUESTION OF BEATITUDE

(Matthew 5:5)

After fire, wild flowers
Everywhere burning bright,
Delicate, slender, strong,
Grace the broad, ashen fields
With purple, pink, and blue,
Bring fragrance to the air,
Herald the cool, moist hope
That stirs beneath the waste,
The charred ruins of lives
Once towering, green, proud.
The conflagration passed,
Nature's vaunt set at naught,
Humbler forms of beauty
Inspire a sudden awe:
Shall the meek inherit
The earth, as has been said?
Are the mighty cast down,
And the lowly raised up
At last? And by what flame?

ALONE I HEAR YOU SPEAK

(*For Paula*)

The wood is solitude of sound and sight,
And here the ear can listen, just as light

Can cut a shaft through limbs and leaves to grass,
To tinge bright gold the quiet green I pass.
Alone, I hear you speak in every blade;
Your voice the glistening hush upon the glade.

ON TAHOE'S STEEP

(The Sierra Nevada Peaks above South Lake Tahoe to the East)

On Tahoe's steep and storm-washed eastern slope
The hemlock, pine, and fir have come to cope,
Even to thrive, with soilless rock for food.
Through centuries of waste these trees have stood
Rock-rooted, sure, drawing sustenance there
Where all that can be seen seems lifeless, bare,
While far below these steepled fastnesses
Lives, weathered less hard, find in trespasses
Of the frontier of the wild and the tame
Their own forms of sustenance: fish and game,
Free play upon the lake. Farther below,
The Sacramento valley, where we grow
Our rice, our soy, our sugar beets, our corn,
All in a fertile soil never outworn,
Washed down from heights long dead, but for the stir
Of wind through rock-fed hemlock, pine, and fir.

THE PRAISE AND THE GLORY

I doubt we'll ever forget
The meadow we passed just yesterday
Tatted with webs dew drenched
And glistening in the sun.
You and I remarked
We'd never seen the like before.
It seemed to us that Charlotte
Must have called a convention of her peers

To fashion, not for us, of course,
But for her and for themselves,
This scene, this acreage of silent praise.
And it came to me,
To you as well, I know,
Though you never spoke of it,
But only smiled your assent:
Who would have thought
That such delicate and unintended art
Should bear such a weight of glory?

CHAPTER THREE

An Essay and Poems
of Ernest Winfield Bartow

WILLIAM STRINGFELLOW: PROFILE OF A
CHRISTIAN RADICAL

BEFORE BEGINNING MY TEACHING career in 1968, I was a Presbyterian pastor. I served two churches, the Prospect Presbyterian Church in Maplewood, New Jersey, and the Bristol Presbyterian Church in Bristol, Pennsylvania. While in the pastorate, I became involved in community outreach, particularly to minority groups. Therefore, when I came upon the writings of a radical Christian lawyer, named William Stringfellow, I was captivated. I was captivated by his Christian radicalism, by his laser focus on the core message of the New Testament: freedom from bondage to the powers and principalities of death. Stringfellow's spiritual journey began with reading the Bible intensely. He found the Bible, particularly the New Testament, eye-opening and transforming. He discovered that Scripture enabled him to see through the deceptively appealing veneer of law, social reform, and political initiative. With regard to Christian mission and witness, Stringfellow allowed for no compromising the demands of the gospel. A young minister in need of finding a voice for a time of pronounced social and political unrest, I was stirred by his unique theological insight and intense public advocacy. In Stringfellow, I found a kindred spirit and timely voice.

While in Bristol, I decided to pursue a ThM degree at Princeton Theological Seminary, where I had already received a master of divinity (MDiv) degree. When it came time for me to choose a subject for my master's thesis, I chose to write about the radical lay theologian and lawyer whose books had already validated my dissatisfaction with American society and the institutional church. A graduate of the London School of Economics and Harvard Law School, Stringfellow moved to Harlem soon after graduating from Harvard to advocate on behalf of the people there who were victims of social marginalization and economic deprivation. Radically biblical, Stringfellow advocated total immersion in Scripture. In the early 1950s, while serving in the armed forces, Stringfellow began seriously, passionately, even desperately, to read the Bible, particularly the New Testament, on his own. In recounting his experience of the word, he writes,

> I remember waking, I remember being freed. I remember being extraordinarily emancipated. So much so, that I first began to love myself, and I believe first began to love others.[1]

At this moment and in this way, the resurrection became an intimate, transforming reality for him. He became a new person, a young lawyer with a new voice and new sense of vocation.

After his almost mystical experience with the word, Stringfellow began seeing the world through a resurrectional lens. With eyes fixed on the words of Scripture, he found abundant evidence that the world in which we live is indeed fallen, a place where death is militant and at work in all things, where, apart from God's work in all things, death is the only meaning there is.

While still in law school, Stringfellow spoke of law in a most unconventional manner. He dared to claim that law originates in hate of God, not in love of God. Few law students would make such a claim. They would see law as remedial, a way of correcting

---

1. Bartow, "Prophet in the Pew," 7.

a wrong, a way of attaining the redress of grievances for those who are unjustly treated. They would not see it, as Stringfellow saw it, as a means of self-justification. In Stringfellow's eyes, the law is necessary only because of the human penchant for lawlessness in a world governed by the powers and principalities of death. He took seriously the brokenness of humanity as exposed in Scripture and regarded the redress of grievances as necessary only because humans are alienated from God and, therefore, from one another.

At the urging of a friend and Presbyterian minister, Stringfellow headed for Harlem after graduating from Harvard. He joined the staff of the East Harlem Protestant Parish and worked there for fifteen months until he resigned. His resignation arose from his unrelenting biblical realism, his insistence on adhering to the uncompromising demands of the gospel. From the start, parish leaders appeared to be confused about the nature of the church and about the parish's mission in Harlem. In his book *My People Is the Enemy* Stringfellow charged that through its first years the parish's mission had become more focused on social reform than on bearing witness to Christian redemption, God's freeing all humanity from the grip of death. He was disturbed that the parish had become too deeply conformed to the world, trusting in their human effort to transform the community and not in the transformative word of God. Stringfellow charged further that there was actually a diffidence toward the word of God that resulted in an "erratic and fortuitous liturgical life in the congregation, dependent upon the personality and whim, even, of the minister presiding at the time," a lack of "concord or confession of faith among either the group's ministry or lay people," and "a radical substitution of conventional charity for the mission of the church."[2]

Stringfellow firmly believed in the autonomy and dynamism of God's word. This belief led him in a very different direction from that of the East Harlem Protestant Parish. He contended that the church's mission in Harlem should be the same as the church's mission anywhere else, which is to celebrate, enjoy, and witness to the Word of God, mediated through the Bible, embodied and exposed in Jesus

2. Bartow, "Prophet in the Pew," 7.

Christ, and present and active in the contemporary world. String-fellow wrote, "The meaning of Jesus Christ is addressed to men, to all men, in the very events and relationships, any and every one of them, which constitutes our existence in the world." While Harlem was undeniably a landscape of death, it was nonetheless in String-fellow's eyes, a community in which God's word was very much alive and moving. Stringfellow's resurrectional realism endowed him with rare perspicacity. Through his intimate association with the poor and disinherited, he found confirmation of the presence and influence of God's word in the lives of all men. He discovered that because the poor live out their lives in such naked proximity to death, the gospel is often anticipated, at least metaphorically, in their street codes. By way of illustration he writes:

> Gang society nurtures a morality which induces mem-
> bers actually to risk their lives for each other and for
> causes which outsiders would think unworthy—like ju-
> risdiction over a street that is filled with garbage or over
> a girl who is probably not a virgin. They risk their lives
> for apparently unworthy purposes.[3]

Within this milieu of suffering and death, Stringfellow was able to discern a prescient, perhaps incipient, Way, Truth, and Life, the reality of Jesus' resurrection.

Stringfellow's trek to Harlem was, in large part, the acting out of his conviction (nurtured in law school) "that the health and maturity of the American legal system depends upon whether or not society's outcasts are, as a practical matter, represented in their rights and complaints before the law."[4] In applying this criterion, he found the American legal system to be neither healthy nor ma-ture. What saddened him most was not that the law was frequently abusive of the poor, but that it was, for the most part, neglectful of the poor. This disregard of the poor not only by the legal com-munity but by mainstream society impelled him to assume an intercessory posture in Harlem. He felt impelled to live with the

3. Bartow, "Prophet in the Pew," 18.
4. Bartow, "Prophet in the Pew," 13.

poor and to risk the vulnerability of the poor because, as he writes, "the venerable ministry of Christians for the poor is not simply for their endurance of hunger or cold or unemployment or illness or rejection by society, but is, at the same time, a way of caring for—interceding for—all others in society who are not poor."[5]

The poverty Stringfellow found in Harlem was dehumanizing to a degree he had never before imagined. The poverty he encountered in his clients was paralyzing deprivation. It was more than a lack of money; it was a life of agony. Born into a working-class family, Stringfellow assumed he knew what poverty was until he confronted the degree of poverty he found in Harlem. The contrast between the poverty he had known as a poor white kid, a member of the white majority in America, and the poverty of poor black kids in Harlem was both astounding and unsettling. Faced with this startling contrast, Stringfellow was forced to confess, "We were poor, but I was not deprived. We were poor, but I could go to college. We were poor, but I was readily accepted in the homes of the rich. We were poor, but I could 'pass' in white bourgeois society. We were poor, but I had a chance."[6] It was easy for Stringfellow to see that the advantages enjoyed by the privileged and powerful were gained at the expense of the poor and forgotten. Stringfellow came to see his move to Harlem as a move in two directions. On the one hand, it was an oblational move, a giving of himself on behalf of the poor, and on the other hand, it was an intercessional move, a flesh and blood entreaty on behalf of his own people, whom he had come to view as the "enemy."

In 1964, President Lyndon Johnson announced his War on Poverty and introduced legislation intended to benefit the poor. While the intent of the legislation was laudable, Stringfellow was quick to point out its many flaws. He contended that it was geared to treat symptoms rather than causes and failed to provide sufficient funding for its lofty goals. He felt it represented a dilettante concern for the poor, an extension of timeworn social remedies that simply would not work. He saw that it curiously benefited

5. Bartow, "Prophet in the Pew," 14–15.
6. Bartow, "Prophet in the Pew," 14–15.

others who were not poor. He saw that it was a pork barrel for local politicians, that it created new positions in the welfare bureaucracy, that it provided a sop for the conscience of the affluent, and that it temporarily distracted the poor from their distress. Stringfellow saw the Great Society legislation as no more a remedy for poverty than putting a Band-Aid on a wound in need of suture.

From Stringfellow's perspective, the major flaw in Johnson's Great Society legislation was its failure to address the potentially ruinous priority given to property rights over human rights. The priority given to property rights, he asserted, traces back to America's agrarian beginnings when the ownership of property was the source of wealth and power. He argued that the priority given property rights is based on the insidious doctrine of self-justification that traces its roots to early forms of Protestantism, which emerged and flourished among owners of land, slave owners, frontier settlers, country people, and pioneer capitalists. The doctrine, as articulated by Stringfellow, is this:

> A man who wills to do so and who dares not to suffer the hindrance of government can perfect his own salvation by the getting, holding, and using of private property. Thus, salvation is not universal nor, in any sense, by God's election but competitive and comes to the man whose worth and worthiness are proved by the property he controls, earns, or owns. To have property is evidence of moral excellence, defines individual dignity, and is the divine reward of self-reliance. In such a view the failure of a man to acquire property not only aborts his personal fulfillment but must be counted as a sin or as a consequence of the interference of evil.[7]

Stringfellow's critique of Johnson's Great Society legislation highlights his engagement with the world. While it reflects the forensic style of a lawyer, Stringfellow's legal background does not fully account for his polemic assault of the *status quo*. His polemical style is more indicative of his being a radical Christian than a radical lawyer. His writing reflects the extreme demands of the

7. Bartow, "Prophet in the Pew," 40.

gospel. It is evidence of the resurrectional perspective he acquired from his experience in the word. The axiom is unassailable: he whose life is a celebration of and witness to the living Christ is he who is free from the intimidation of death and, thereby, a citizen of the city of salvation, which God has created. Those who inhabit the city of God are necessarily aliens in the cities of this fallen world. The gulf between those who inhabit the city of God and those who inhabit a city of their own creation is the gulf between grace and self-justification, the gulf between life and death. Stringfellow's message echoed the voice of the apostle Paul, "Do not be conformed to this world but be transformed by the renewal of your mind that you may prove what is the will of God" (Rom 12:2).

BIRTH OF AN ADULT CHILD

A nine-year-old child,
I lived in my imagination
And played many roles:
Pistol-packin' cowboy,
Swashbuckling pirate,
Sharp-shooting commando.
I was always daring,
Always invincible,
Until I heard the doctor's voice
Outside my bedroom door:
"We have to operate now
Or he might not make it through the fall."
His words like bullets
Pierced the cowboy,
The pirate,
The commando,
And the child
Who could no longer
Be daring,
Invincible,
Or nine.

THE SPIRIT OF UKRAINE

She sweeps up shards of glass,
As the earth shakes beneath her feet,
And she sings her country's national anthem.
Bombs fall and buildings collapse
Along with the values and aspirations
Once held dear by freedom fighters everywhere.
Be not misled by her tear-filled eyes.
An intrepid freedom fighter,
She holds tight invincible dreams
That strengthen her resolve to carry on,
Despite all that portends democracy's end.
Look up, America, and see her
Through the cybernetic fog
That obscures rancor grown viral,
And discover anew
The source of invincible dreams.

DREAMS AT WAR

Bombs explode,
The earth trembles,
Buildings collapse,
And a father sobs
At the feet of his teenage son
Whose future is denied
By a madman,
Determined to realize
The impossible dream
Of conquering a people
Who dare dream
Of keeping the freedom
They now defiantly protect,
Never to be denied.

KING

Your name was your stature,
As you walked humbly among us,
Speaking of dignity,
Born of character.
And justice,
Born of peaceful protest.

As you move graveward this day,
You ride upon a mule-drawn cart
With dignity money can't buy
In your final freedom march.

Gandhi, your sword,
Christ, your light,
You battled oppression
From jail
With unrelenting forgiveness
And sowed the seeds
Of a dream
Now reaped in liberating death.

"Free at last,
Free at last,
Thank God almighty,
I'm free at last."

AUDACIOUS HOPE

A tribute to Barack Obama

Years ago, a dream was born
And found a voice
Too soon stilled but not forgotten.
The voice rang out
With promise of freedom
For those long bound
By chains, unseen but sorely felt,

64

And for those long shackled
By ignorance and fear.
The voice was stilled
But the vision endures,
As the fragile seed of hope, deeply planted
In the soil of the human heart,
Awaits the proper clime
To bring promise to bloom.

Today, another voice is heard,
Echoing the dreamer's dream,
Daring to promise, "Yes, we can,"
Tilling soil and watering seed.

GEORGE FLOYD'S LAST BREATH
(In memoriam)

Handcuffed, arms secured
Behind his back,
A black man cries,
"I can't breathe,"
As he feels the press
Of animus against his neck
Until he breathes no more.

Knee or noose,
Cop or klansman,
It matters not
To those who feel
The weight of their forebears' chains
And carry the wounds
Of their forebears' fate.
They too cry, "I can't breathe.
I can't breathe the air you breathe
Drink the water you drink,
Walk the streets you walk,
Live where you live,

Or learn where you learn.
I am an alien
With different skin,
Different hair,
And different speech.
I live behind an invisible wall
Over which you cannot see me
Or hear my voice,
Even as I cry out for life.
You cannot feel the weight
Of my forebears' chains
Or feel the pain
Of my forebears' fate
And so I cry
And long for breath."

Days, weeks, months, and years
Have passed,
And still few hear us
Or see us as we are
Or themselves as they are.
What will unstop the ears
Of those who share the deafness
Of the unheeding cop
And open the eyes
Of those who cannot see
Beyond the invisible wall?
When will they hear us cry,
"I can't breathe?"

TO JOHN

(In memory of John Lennon)

Bird of Liverpool,
Abandoned early in your nest,
You tried your wings before most do,

Eager to fly high above
Cities, towns, villages, and ports
Into an open, boundless sky
Where you could circle the world
And make it listen.
Upon the upward draft of song,
You soared above all others of your kind
And claimed a generation as your own.
Uneasy still, at this new height,
You sought in lyric dreams
To rise a quantum more
Above rude and hostile winds
To claim the yet unclaimed,
Till claimed by love
You came to nest in your adopted city home
Where, one dark night,
Madness had its way
And stilled the bird
Who lately sang,
"Give peace a chance."

THE HOMELESS WOMAN

She sits on a park bench
In the shade of an old tree,
A comfortable place
At least for now.
Disheveled and dressed in overworn clothes,
Her body, still as stone,
Her face, a mask of despair,
She stares ahead transfixed,
Unmindful of passersby,
Equally detached and indifferent.
In the tree above,
A bird moves from branch to branch,
And questions fly into my mind.

Who is this woman?
What is she thinking?
From whence did she come?
Where will she be going next?
I dare not ask,
But I wonder
And feel uneasy
As I look ahead toward nightfall
And the moment I go to bed at home
And the woman retires
To some unknown, barren space
As the bird returns to its nest.

PESTILENCE 1 (AIDS)

She whose ways prevail
Sweeps with an indifferent broom
Through a chaotic house.
Coarse bristles assault
The unsuspecting young,
Their future, a cloud,
Their promise, waste,
Despite all ties and pressing need,
Despite all science, care, and prayer.
We who grow old
Stare, wondering, at clocks
And choke upon the airborne
Dust of hope.

PESTILENCE 2 (COVID-19)

She whose ways prevail
Sweeps with an indifferent broom
Through a chaotic house.
Coarse bristles randomly assault

The unsuspecting old,
The unsuspecting young,
The unsuspecting rich,
The unsuspecting poor.
Distinctions blur
As fevers spike
And helpless victims
Under linen shrouds,
Gasp for breath
And struggle to hold fast
Their fragile dreams
Of life ahead.

We, who sit alone,
Anxious and perplexed,
Stare, wondering, at clocks
And choke on the airborne dust of hope.

POST 9/11 ANTHEM

Light shines still from our Lady's torch,
Our flags fly high and proud,
And spirits soar on wings of song
As we sing, strong and loud.

America holds firm still.
Her fields of grain still wave.
Her purple mountains, still in place,
Embrace the strong and brave.

We'll sing on, America
As long as we draw breath.
We'll sing of all that we hold dear
And faithful be to death.

America, America,
Your wounds are healing fast.
Songs and prayers fill the air,

And we're renewed at last.

Let's move on, America,
Determined to ever be
The light of hope, shining bright,
For all the world to see.

THIS OLD HOUSE

I've lived in this house since birth,
But it no longer feels like home.
It provides neither comfort nor ease,
And offers little protection,
As years pass and bring unwelcome changes.
A compassionless mirror
Reveals the damage done by years of wear and tear
In spite of all mitigating efforts.
Days of quick repairs and restorations
Have given way to days of unending maintenance.
In spite of all it suffers,
The old house still stands,
But for how long?
There is no telling.
There are only days
Of anxious waiting
And rescuing distractions.

THE RETIREMENT HOME

I arise one morning,
And sunlight greets me
As I open the blinds and look out.
Promises to be a cloudless day, I think,
Until I open the exit door
And find a hearse parked outside,
Between my building and the next,

Waiting to receive yet another victim of mortality.
Mortality fills the corridors here
Where residents shuffle along with canes and walkers
And peer through the fog of age.
Here, memory fades and time is lost.
Here, dependence is feared; independence, coveted.
Here, pleasantries mask quiet unease,
And smiles conceal silent suffering.
Here, my infirmities are mirrored daily
And old notions die.

WALKING WESTWARD

I walk westward
As the sun begins its descent
And I glance backward
To find my shadow
Stretching behind me
On the eventful path
I now walk, and I wonder
What of me will lie behind,
After the sun sets one last time,
And my shadow is but a trail
Of memories.

HOLDING ON

I feel November's chill as I look up at a solitary leaf
Hanging from the branch of an oak,
Defiant of winter's threatening approach.
Having fed the mighty tree,
In the season of its growth,
This leaf must be soon shed
And join those already on the ground below,
But not yet.

Stubborn to the end,
This leaf hangs on,
Fighting the icy wind's assault,
Holding on for one more day, maybe more.
And here I am at eighty-five,
Standing below and looking up,
Awestruck and resolute.

ENNUI

Shady Elm, they call it,
Mortuary for the living,
Geriatric nursery
For those destined to endure
A second infancy.
Ensconced in linen,
They wait and wait and wait,
And wonder what each day will bring.
A letter perhaps?
A visitor?
Marmalade on my toast?
Who knows?
Maybe that fly will return to my window,
Maybe the nurse will stumble and spill my tea.
Maybe the weary rose on my night stand
Will last another day.
Maybe this day will be my . . .
No, not likely.
I'm getting too anxious.
The hour has not yet come.
I can still feed myself
Without dropping a crumb.

THE WORD

In the beginning was the Word, and the Word was with God, and the Word was God.
John 1:1

He who does not love does not know God; for God is love.
1 John 4:8

In the beginning was the Word,
Only the Word and nothing more,
No sky or stars,
No earth or waters,
No fish or fowl
Until the Word spoke
And called forth
The sky and stars,
Earth and waters,
Fish and fowl.
The Word speaks still
And calls forth
New planets and stars
To fill the never ending space beyond.
Ever far yet ever near,
The Word shares with us
The power to express and create
And joins us amidst the turmoil
Of our failed creation,
This desert of separation,
To lead us into the garden of
Oneness with the Word
And with all others
In need of filling
With the love that creates anew.

BIRTH OF AN OUTCAST STAR

The time had come
To give Caesar his due: taxes,
The inexorable scourge of citizenship,
The burden of all who walk
In darkness, the darkness East of Eden,
Where gold and silver,
Tempt, mislead, and corrupt.

Bethlehem was overrun,
No lodging available,
All rooms taken,
"No Vacancy" signs everywhere.
A stable would have to do,
A stable filled with beasts of burden,
Creatures born to bear and serve.

Destined to bear and serve,
He brought light like no other
Into a darkness like no other,
A light first seen only by outcasts and aliens,
A light that shines still upon the path
To a garden long lost.

FOR ONE BEREAVED

When death assails,
Love prevails
For those who dare believe
That death is dead
And not the one
Whose passing you now grieve.
Death is darkness,
Love is light,
And love shall soon dispel
The darkness of your loss,

And help you see that all is well,
That deep within your heart
Survives a bond much too strong
For death to break apart.

PRISONER OF PANIC

Suddenly, I feel menaced
By something beyond or within,
I'm not sure.
My heart races,
I gasp for breath,
Death looms,
Or so it seems.
I want to run
But where?
I need help
But from whom?
I run for a cover and wait
For a moment of fragile peace
And transient calm.

I lie in bed at home,
Shades drawn.
My bedroom, a tomb,
Shuts out the noisy,
Disturbing world beyond.
I feel safe for now,
But a menace lurks
In the shadows
And fear holds me captive.

In a cold, sterile place,
I lie in bed, drugged and numbed,
Still a prisoner
Wondering what awaits me
As doctors discuss my case

And plan my path
To freedom.

ERNIE'S SALUTE TO ERNIE

It's Sunday, our Happy Hour,
And here we are again,
You and I,
Old and forever one,
With no one else
To share this quiet space
And speak of things
Beyond these cloistering walls.

We no longer stand tall
And walk securely
Among those engaged, day by day,
In work and play,
Dreaming dreams we once dreamed.
Loving someone special as once we did,
Celebrating life as we once knew it.

We are cloistered now, Yes,
But not imprisoned.
The mind we share still soars,
And our imagining has no limits.
We still live as we choose to live
And do what we choose to do.
So I raise my glass to us,
Seasoned, intrepid warriors,
Who still fight the troubling ghosts
We have always fought,
And still scale the unseen walls
We have always scaled,
Determined to stay the course
We've long been on.

HERE'S TO EBEN FLOOD: A response to Edwin Arlington Robinson's "Mr. Flood's Party"

Yes, Mr. Flood,
Life ebbs and flows,
But it is the ebbing
I now feel
As you did
When you partied
With yourself
That lonely besotted night
With only two moons
To hear you sing
Farewell to years past.

Farewell, I say
To friends who used to call
And those with whom
I used to sing goodbye
To years shared,
Well spent,
And now gone.
This Sunday, I shall party too
And sip a drink
I've prepared and poured,
Then toast all
Who suffer time's
Cruel thievery.

I know not what lies in store
As time speeds ahead
And leaves me
Breathless in its wake.

Days pass
And as they do,
The sun looks dimmer
And clouds look darker.

Vision dims
As the past grows longer
And the future, shorter,
And memories replace
Lost friends.
Here's to you, Mr. Flood!

ON WORD OF MY FIRST GRANDCHILD

Tiffani

God said to Moses, "I am who I am," and he said, "Say this to the people of Israel, I am has sent me to you." (Exod 3:14)

A mystery forms within you, dear Lisa,
Taking on bone and flesh,
Gaining definition,
Moving more day by day,
Neurons and ganglia
Already sending and receiving
As cells in darkness
Move steadily toward light,
Preparing to issue forth as I am,
The I am you shall name and care for,
The I am who shall wonder who I am is,
The I am who shall wonder what I am means,
The I am who shall meet others who say I am,
And share this strange perplexing place
Where question leads to question without end
And I am keeps becoming
More than neurons and ganglia,
More than bone and flesh,
Attending or denying or ignoring the deep that calls to deep,
Preparing for an end or a beginning.

FOR TIFFANI ON THE OCCASION OF HER COLLEGE GRADUATION

Years ago, grandfather-to-be,
I wrote a poem
About a child, yet unborn, yet unnamed,
Destined to join the company
Of those who affirm their being
With the words, "I am."
Once born, then named
That grandchild soon found a voice
With which to say, "I am Tiffani"
And later to say
"I am a woman,
I am a wife,
I am a mother
I am a student,
I am a college graduate."

Diploma in hand,
She now moves ahead
With hopes and dreams
Yet to be realized,
Surrounded by love
Uplifted by prayer,
And strengthened by faith.

Love,
Pop-Pop
May 12, 2018

BOX 12

Baby bluebirds chirp in vain from their nesting box,
Crying for their ill-fated parents
Whose wings and feathers lie on the ground below,
Spare scraps of a predator's meal.

We mourn our treasured friends' painful loss
And call for help in keeping fragile hope alive.
Rescued and receiving care in their new home,
Our avian friends live on, their infant hearts still beating
Beneath feathered breasts but not for long.
The hour comes too soon when the beating stops
And all is lost or so it seems to us
Who live on for now and wait in vain
For answers to questions
Ever asked by those who grieve.

FRIENDSHIP

What strange mixture of choice and chance
Keeps friends together through time and circumstance?
What explains the weblike strength of their bonding?
Why is their talk never idle,
And their silence never empty?
Who can tell us why in their letting go
They find themselves and each other?
Friends are bound by an alchemy no other can explain.
Their bonding needs no explanation;
It is simply theirs to enjoy
And in their sharing,
Create a world all their own.

COUNTDOWN

The years grow colder
As we move our separate ways,
Barely mindful that the path
We started upon
Divided when we weren't looking.
Now wrapped in busyness,
We stare across a foreboding space

That keeps growing.

A fire once crackled between us,
Its radiance mirrored in our eyes,
It's warmth shared and enjoyed.
We played games for fun,
And moments of silence
Were never awkward or empty.

Sadly, all that once was is now lost.
We no longer play games for fun, just winning,
And we are fearful of silence
Since the unattended fire has died away,
And our days are full
Of pretending.

THE REALIST

The realist looks through an uncommon lens
And sees shades of grey
Where others see black or white,
Speaks of "both-and," not "either-or,"
And expects the unexpected
In an ever-changing world of randomness.
Always questioning
And bedeviled with doubts,
The realist walks through the mist of ambiguity
And endures the discomfort of uncertainty.

SPRING

Dressed in green apparel
With accents of lilac and yellow,
She greets me under a canopy of blue,
And I breathe in the fresh, sweet, perfume
That always signals her presence.
Each year, she arrives on time

And awakens senses,
Grown dormant under winter's blanket,
With the welcome rush of sprouting.

LIFEGUARD

With crown of sun-bleached hair,
Shoulders broad as a rowing scull,
And muscles, smooth as sand dunes,
He sits upon his elevated throne
And keeps watch over his "surfdom,"
While sun-tanned subjects
Pay homage to yet another ruler in the sky.

And the surf pounds on.

Beneath the throne of this sun-kissed king,
Giggling beach nymphs
Compete for his attention
While he dreams of the pleasures
Of the coming night
When the moon takes rule of sky
And high tide shifts to low.

And the surf pounds on.

At summer's end,
His rule over,
The surf pounds still
And sand castles,
Abandoned and forgotten,
Vanish.

CHAPTER FOUR

Resurrection

An Opera in Two Acts

Introductory Remarks

As a preaching pastor and teacher of preaching pastors from 1963 until my last class as adjunct professor of speech communication emeritus at Princeton Theological Seminary in the second semester of the 2017 academic year, I have had the great honor and privilege of participating in various projects under the direction of extraordinary musicians. I will not list them all. Some are well known in the world of music generally, and in the world of sacred music particularly. In my octogenarian years all of those names, faces, talents come vividly to mind. My recent collaboration with Dr. Paul S. Undreiner, composer of the opera *Resurrection* therefore, may be considered as at once the climax and the dénouement of these, for me, ever-living moments of creative endeavor.

The opera *Resurrection*, exegetically grounded in a close reading of chapter 20 of the Gospel according to John in the context of the Johannine witness as a whole, was Paul Undreiner's idea. He asked me on a Tuesday night after choir practice to write the libretto. I was startled. I had never imagined considering such a formidable undertaking. As Paul himself was aware, and as I reminded him, there were professional librettists who might be willing to take on the assignment. But Paul insisted that he wanted a librettist who, in fact, believed John's Gospel account of the resurrection of Jesus Christ, our Lord. I took a week to consider Paul's request. At last I decided to give it a try. Here, then, you have the results of his offer and my acceptance of it. Our work together was, certainly for me, a joyful attempt at "from faith for faith" (Rom 1:6) proclamation of the gospel in operatic form. We undertook our attempt prayerfully, confident that our just and compassionate Savior would overrule any sin and error contained in the opera or in the performing or hearing of it. The exegetical, theological, technical, and formal poetic considerations I had to take into account in writing the libretto were legion, for they were many. Detailing them here, however, would be tedious for those not deeply interested in such matters and redundant for those all too familiar with what these concerns might be.

Therefore, I will wrap up these introductory remarks with a word of thanks to Dr. Paul S. Undreiner, my choir director (my wife, Paula, and I both sing under his direction). Paul is an organist, virtuoso pianist, composer, and university graduate school instructor in music (formally with the Mason Gross School for the Arts, at Rutgers University, New Brunswick, New Jersey). Paul's knowledge of music history and theory is astonishing. Furthermore, he is a past master of musical interpretation of biblical and poetic literature. Above all he is a happy Christian of deep piety. He prays without ceasing and walks in his integrity. He is my friend.

Resurrection was twice performed as an operatic oratorio with Paul Undreiner at the piano and conducting. The soloists who sang the arias and the recitatives and short spoken texts were professionals. Choir members of First Presbyterian Church, Ramsey, New Jersey, took part in the performance of the chorales. There are three hymn texts in the libretto that church congregants may sing to well-known tunes. The vesper hymn "O Word of Joy and Gladness" may be sung to the tune *Aurelia*, the musical setting for "The Church's One Foundation." The hymn "Despite a Darkened World Around" may be sung to the familiar tune of "Amazing Grace." The Easter Sunday trinitarian hymn "O Word of God, O

Life's True Light" may be sung to the tune "Quebec," "Jesus, Thou Joy of Loving Hearts." Let the communion of saints everywhere and in everything from grief to gladness ever sing! Hallelujah! The Lord God omnipotent reigns!

Text of RESURRECTION

Paul S. Undreiner—Composer
Charles L. Bartow—Librettist

ACT I—Scene 1

Mary's Thoughts on Her Way to Jesus' Garden Tomb

To me your words were light in deepest night,
Expelling demon threats and sick'ning fears,
And pointing out the way that I should go
To apprehend the presence of my God
In love as strong as death, and tender yet
As all-forgiving, all embracing care.

O blessed Rabbi, Jesus, teach me still,
Despite your cruel end on Golgotha,
To claim your promised peace to ease my grief.
O Life! O Love! Sustain me as I walk
This cheerless, dark, and long sepulchral hour.

Ahead I see the garden tomb, the stone—
The stone! The stone is rolled aside, and who,
Oh! Who has taken you away, and where?
I must tell John and Peter, "Come and see!"
God grant me speed!

Mary Magdalene to Peter and John

Peter! John!
This first day of the week—
It still was dark—
I came to our Lord's tomb.
The stone was rolled aside!
They took away the Lord out of the tomb,
And we do not know where they laid him.

Trio: Mary, Peter, John

Mary: Your words to me were light in deepest night.
          O Life! O Love! O Lord!
          I yearn to see you still,
          If only in your grave clothes lying there.
          But you've been tak'n away, and who knows where?

Peter: What can this mean, your grave clothes laid aside,
          O Life, O Love, O Lord?!
          Your words—eternal life—
          Though you are gone, silenced, still echo here.
          What's come of you? And what's to come of us?

John: I see and I believe you've conquered death!
          O Life, O Love, O Lord,
          For us, for all, you said:
          "I am the resurrection and the life;
          Those who believe in me shall never die."
          (John 19:25–26)

ACT 1—Scene 2

Mary (weeping)

My tears shall be my food now, day and night,
While others taunt me: "Where, where is your God?"

For Jesus, my beloved Rabbi, Lord
My healer, whom I long have served with joy—
From back home by the sea of Galilee,
Up to this very spot where I must mourn
The loss of him, all trace of him removed—
Was hung on Golgotha, where I stood by
With mother, Mary, watching death come on.
Yet here the smell of death itself seems gone
Without a trace! How strange this darkness is
At dawn! How strange as well the brightening day!
It seems an inextinguishable light,
The very light of life! And from the tomb,
A twinned white, beck'ning radiance appears!
Despite my tears, I must seek out its source.

Trio: Mary, Angel 1, Angel 2

Mary: Two figures, dazzling white
               Are seated where my Lord
               Was laid: one at his head,
               One at his feet, just so,
               An apparition! Now
               They speak as angels speak,
               As messengers divine.

Angels: Questioning Mary

Angel 1: You're weeping, tell us why.
Angel 2: Why are you weeping here
Angel 1: Before this empty tomb
Angel 2: That's bright'ning with the dawn,
Angels 1 and 2: The very light of life?

Mary: Responding to the Angels' Questioning

They've tak'n away my Lord,
I know not where or why.
Despite this bright'ning day,
I weep the very light
Of life he seemed to me.

Trio: Mary, Angels 1 and 2

Angels 1 and 2: This empty tomb, once dark,
Fills with the bright'ning day,
Inextinguishable light!
It is the very light of life!

Mary: This empty tomb, once dark,
Fills with the bright'ning day.
Inextinguishable light!
He seemed, the very light of life!

Duet: Mary, Jesus

Jesus: Woman, why are you weeping?
Whom are you looking for?

Mary: O gard'ner, Sir, I'm weeping
For they've tak'n away my Lord.
If you have laid him somewhere,
Tell me where you have laid him;
And I will take him away.

Jesus: Mary!

Mary: Rabbi!

Jesus: Mary, do not hold me,
I've not yet ascended
To the Father.

But go to my brothers,
And say to them:
I am ascending
To my Father
And your Father,
To my God
And your God.

Jesus Prays to His Father

O Father whom I love and long for so,
So long I've been away from heav'n my home,
To you I'll soon return, my work here done,
Your work of saving love for all the world.
The overflowing love of God is theirs,
Whose love for me has drawn them to yourself,
And stirred in them belief and trust in me
For life eternal as the life we share,
My resurrection not all mine alone,
But promise of their resurrection too,
That they, and you, and I, might all be one.

As Mary just now heard me speak her name,
And recognized me in the voice she heard,
So shall all know me Shepherd of their lives,
Who hear in voices echoing my tone,
The voice of their Good Shepherd, Rabbi, friend,
Their light in darkness, trial, and martyrdom.

Turning from Prayer to Those Listening:

"I am the resurrection and the life.
Do you believe this?"

Mary; Chorale: Ensemble

Mary: O blessed Peter, O beloved John,
                    Disciples dear, all brothers of my Lord:
                    I've seen the Lord. He said to tell you this:
                    "I am ascending to my Father
                    And your Father,
                    To my God and your God."

Ensemble: Mary, Disciples:

O word of joy and gladness,
Of light, and life, and love,
Good news to quell our sadness,
Peace sent us from above!
Jesus our Lord is risen
O'er all the world to reign.
Despite night-fears we're given
Courage to praise his name.
Yet still we're filled with yearning
Once more to see his face
And hear his voice still burning
Into our hearts God's grace:
The grace of sins forgiven
Of souls set free for love,
Clouds of injustice riven
By heav'ns descending dove.
The vesper hours are nearing,
The hours of evensong.
God grant our Lord's appearing
Will cheer us here ere long.
Our Holy Savior's greeting,
His call, "All hail and peace!"
Will make our nightfall meeting
A resurrection feast!

ACT II—Scene 1

Peter: Those who crucified the Lord
        Also threaten us with death.
        Therefore shut and bolt the door
        Lest from fear we find no rest.

All: There is a deeper darkness
        Than this now descended night,
        Such a darkness as inhibits
        All glad welcoming of light,
        Such light as Mary spoke of
        When she said, "I've seen the Lord!"

John: Such light as I was blessed with
        At the empty tomb this morn,
        In love believing promised
        Love and life from Christ our Lord.

Andrew: Remember—at the temple—
        Before his appointed time,
        How he faced the evil pow'rs
        Lurking still outside this door,
        How he said to one and all,
        "I am the light of the world,"
        And, "Whoever follows me
        Will never walk in darkness
        But will have the light of life?"

All: Yes, all this we recall.

Peter: Let us pray and sing to God,
        Our light and our salvation,
        Pray and sing—in Jesus' name.

All: How precious is your steadfast
        love, O God!
        All people may take refuge in
        the shadow of your wings.

For with you is the fountain of life;
In your light we see light.

Jesus: Peace be with you—my brothers.
          Here, see my hands and side.
          It is truly I myself.
          The crucified is risen
          Vanquishing powr's of darkness,
          Conquering both sin and death.

Peter: Already all our dark fears
          Are abating! Our Rabbi
          And our Lord restored to us!
          Hallelujah!

Disciple 1, Peter: Praise the Lord!

Disciple 2: Praise God in his sanctuary;
          3: Praise him in his mighty firmament;
          4: Praise him for his mighty deeds;
          5: Praise him according to his surpassing greatness!
          6: Praise him with trumpet sound;
          7: Praise him with lute and harp!
          8: Praise him with tambourine and dance,
          9: Praise him with strings and pipe!
          10: Praise him with clanging cymbals;
          Praise him with loud crashing cymbals!

All: Let everything that breathes praise the Lord!
          Praise the Lord!
          Hallelujah! (Ps 150, with "Hallelujah" of Martin Lu-
          ther's German translation)

Jesus: My brothers! Peace be with you/
          As the Father has sent me,
          Even so do I send you.
          My father gave to Adam
          Breath for earthly human life,
          But with the Holy Spirit,
          You receive from me heav'ns life,

93

Life shared with God, my Father.
This breath in you is power
To forgive sins in my name.
But if any, in contempt,
Despise proffered forgiveness,
Their sins against the Father,
Son, and Spirit are retained.
Peace I leave with you, my peace.
Henceforth do not live in fear.

Let not your hearts be troubled,
Neither let them be afraid!

Peter: We'll meet again next Lord's Day eve.
           And Thomas will be with us then.

All: Despite a darkened world around
           And terrors to dismay,
           Christ's faith, and hope, and love abound
           And light salvation's way.

           Salvation's way is peace, truth, life,
           Christ's Father's will obeyed,
           Defeat of envy, hatred, strife,
           Dark pow'rs of evil stayed.

           Proclaim forgiveness far and wide
           Declare sin's captives free!
           Leave no one upon earth denied
           Tidings of victory.

           The vict'ry of the crucified
           O'er death and hell in scope,
           Is glad news ev'n for those who've died,
           Is resurrection hope!

ACT II—Scene 2

Thomas: I am alone and will to be alone
           As he, alone, by hate was crucified,

Though I was certain we'd all share his fate:
"Let us also go, that we may die with him,"
I said, when Jesus started out for Bethany,
A stone's throw from Jerusalem and pow'rs
Arrayed against "the way, the truth, the life"
He taught and lived, and counseled us to live.
But my brave resolution now is mocked
As he was taken, mocked, and crucified,
He, himself, alone: "The hour is coming.
Indeed it has come," he said, "when you will
Be scattered, each one to his home, and you
Will leave me alone." We left him alone.
And now I am alone, alone and lost.

(a knock at the door)

Thomas: Who is there?

Peter: Peter

John: John

All disciples: All your brothers, brothers of our Lord.

Peter: Peace be with you Thomas!

Thomas: Your greeting is a painful irony.
How can we share a peace we have not got?
We were scattered, as our Lord said we'd be,
Each to his own home. He was left alone
To face the pow'rs of darkness, fear, and death,
Of sacred trust betrayed to keep the peace,
Just as the world keeps peace, quiet as death.
He bore the cross that seemed his destiny:
The high priest made it clear, and argued well:
"Is it not better one man die
Than the whole nation be destroyed?"
So our Lord died to keep the peace Rome's way.
But peace with God, our soul's joy, we're denied.

Disciples: We've seen the Lord. "Peace be with you," he said.

Peter: The cross he bore was God's strange victory
                O'er death and darkness, fear, betrayal, guilt!

John: O Thomas, brother, you are not alone.
                With you we'll see our Lord again, and soon,
                The evening of the first day of the week
                Upcoming, and in dark Jerusalem.

Thomas: How can this be?
                Unless I see the mark of the nails in his hands,
                And put my finger in the mark of the nails,
                And my hand in his side, I will not believe!

ACT II—Scene 3

Peter, John, Thomas, Disciples, Jesus

Peter: We meet again behind closed doors,
                Expectant now and not in fear,
                For in the darkness round about
                Light shines, the very light of life.
                We've seen the crucified alive,
                And so will see him yet again.

John: We'll see him as his love for us,
                Stronger than death, stirs love of him.
                He promised, "I will love them,
                And reveal myself to them."

Disciples
(but not Thomas): He was crucified for us
                    Under Pontius Pilate
                    But the tree he died upon
                    He made the tree of life.
                    Hallelujah!

Jesus: Peace be with you.
                Thomas, put your finger here,
                See my hands, reach out your hand

And put it in my side.
Do not doubt but believe.

Thomas: My Lord and my God.

Jesus: Thomas, have you believed
Because you have seen me?
Blessed are those who've not seen
And yet have come to believe.

Blessed are those who come to believe
Because of your testimony
As to what you've seen and believed.

Now you are my apostles
Sent to tell the world God's love.
For God so loved the world
That he gave his only begotten Son
That everyone who believes in him
Should not perish but have eternal life.
And this is eternal life
That they may know the only true God,
And Jesus Christ whom God has sent.

Duet, Jesus and Thomas alternating

Jesus: I am the light of the world.
Whoever follows me
Will never walk in darkness
But will have the light of life.

Thomas: You are the light of the world.
Once I walked in darkness
All alone and in despair.
But now I've the light of life.

All disciples: The light shines in the darkness
And the darkness cannot overcome it.

Jesus: I am the Word

That in the beginning
Was with God and was God.

Thomas: You are God's Word,
My way, my truth, my life,
Eternal life. What Joy!

All disciples: The light shines in the darkness
And the darkness cannot overcome it.

Jesus: No one has ever seen God.
The only begotten Son
Alone has declared him.

Thomas: God, whom no one's ever seen
You reveal to me, Lord Christ,
Crucified and risen.

All disciples: The light shines in the darkness

(and Thomas) And the darkness cannot overcome it
Praise the Lord!
Hallelujah!

Jesus: Soon I must ascend to God, my Father.
As before I said to you: "It is to your
Advantage that I go away, for if I do
Not go away, the advocate will not come
To you. I will send the advocate to you,
Even the Spirit of truth, and he will
Guide you into all the truth; for he will
Not speak on his own, but will speak
Whatever he hears from God, my Father,
And from me. He will glorify me,
Because he will take what is mine
And declare it to you.
Father, I have glorified you
By finishing the work you
Gave me to do. And now, O Father,
Glorify me in you own presence
With the glory I had in your presence
Before the world existed."

Epilogue: Concluding Hymn

O Word of God, O life's true light,
Piercing the darkness, quick'ning sight,
Grant us, despite our doubt and fear
A vision of God's glory near.
Condemned to die on Pilate's tree,
A spectacle for all to see,
You made of that curs'd tree's despair
A fount of light and sin's repair.
The Resurrection and the Life,
Bestowing peace amidst earth's strife,
You send your Spirit, Holy Dove,
A flame of truth and steadfast love.
Jesus, Messiah, God's own Son
Whose vict'ry o'er the grave has won
Deliverance from death, guilt, shame,
Give life to us in your dear name.

And let our glad songs ever be
To God, the Holy Trinity:
To Father, Son, and Spirit true,
One God, to whom all praise is due.

Afterword
Humility and Empathy

IN HIS *INSTITUTES OF the Christian Religion*, Calvin insisted that the essence of the Christian life is "humility, humility, humility."[1] Preaching and poetry undertaken in an attempt to faithfully bear witness to life—to the Life that is Life Indeed, to human life as it is actually lived, and to the life of the world around as it may be seen and felt—therefore (and all the more certainly!) needs to be undertaken prayerfully and with humility. All art—preaching and poetry, prose and drama, musical art, operatic art, all performance art and visual art—if it is to be "from faith for faith," (i.e., "art for faith's sake"), must be a humble, not a boastful quest. Following the thought of the apostle Paul, if there is to be any boasting at all or glorying, let it be a boasting in and of the Lord (2 Cor 10:17). For God is the artist of the "Real," as Barrett Browning has written. In the "Real," God and God's truth are revealed. And if human creativity of any sort is to be thought of as in the divine image, as Dorothy Sayers insists,[2] it must seek to be conformed to the truth of what that image entails. And it can never entail a presumption of a status akin to God. We do not imagine God (however much we inevitably must and do speak of God in human terms). It is God who imagines and creates us human beings in his image. Whatever else the *imago dei* means, it means this certainly:

1. Calvin, *Institutes*, 268–69.
2. Sayers, "Zeal of Thy House," 339.

that we human beings stand in relation to God as creatures to the Creator. A popular thought contends that people can and should constantly "reinvent" themselves. But we haven't invented or created ourselves in the first place. If there is reinventing of us to be done, it will be God's reinventing, God's remaking of us. God has done and is doing this. It is called sanctification in and through Jesus Christ. In Christ we find true humanity, the *imago dei*, as God intended it to be from the beginning. The *imago dei* in us therefore is Christ in us in the power of the Holy Spirit, "Christ in you," the apostle Paul insists, "the hope of glory" (Col 1:27). And being remade by God, God's restoring us to what it means to be made in his image, provides the hope of a glorious remaking of the entire creation. This includes what is commonly called the "natural order" (Rom 8:19–21).

In her remarkable, memorable publication *Preaching As Theology and Art* Elizabeth Achtemeier tells us this is so. She also shows us *how* this is so with her sermons. She illustrates with great skill what it means to attempt preaching as theology and art. Read especially her sermon "God the Music Lover."[3] Read the sermon with your mind's ear alert to the sound and feel of it. An embodied hearing of Achtemeier's from faith for faith witness to life draws us all *out of ourselves*, so to speak, and into fellowship with the God who was and is everlastingly creative. And it draws us into caring relationships with all God has created, and is recreating.

Humble artistic endeavor of any sort requires empathy, a coming to terms with, and so, coming to know, something of the life of others and of the Other. As Edward Dowey made clear, Calvin was convinced that we could not know very much even of ourselves, let alone anybody or anything else in the created order, apart from the knowledge of God as God makes Godself known to us.[4] But *deus cognitus, deus nullus*, H. H. Farmer has reminded us, is our reality. That is to say, a God comprehended is no God and the theology—or the artistic endeavor—that pretends

---

3. Achtemeier, *Preaching*, 62–70.

4. Dowey, *Knowledge of God*, 66–68; 146–47.

to comprehension of God is a sham.[5] Likewise our knowledge of others, our empathic coming to terms with them, as they reveal themselves to us, never leads to comprehension. I have been married to my wife, Paula, for nearly sixty years. And a good deal of what she thinks and feels I can think and feel with her. I can even say that I can understand her and how she has come upon her thoughts and feelings concerning the things in her life that matter to her. Yet I do not, and never will, comprehend her. I will never be able to wrap my mind around all that she is and can mean to herself, to me, to others. Only the great Searcher of Hearts can do that (e.g., Ps 139). And the great Searchers of Hearts has done that. God possesses aseity. God is sufficient unto Godself. Yet, too, in a wonderful letter to me regarding his reading of one of my poems, theologian Daniel Migliore reminded me that we need to speak of God's *proseity*, his ever-reaching out to us and to all created things with the love that will not let us go. Through the self-giving of God we know God. Through God's self-giving God knows us better than we know ourselves, comprehends us in all our frailty and vulnerability. And, despite knowing us through and through, God wants us, cares for us. And if we have wandered off indifferent to all that self-giving of God and God's wanting of us, God does not give up on us. Instead, God welcomes us upon our return (see Luke 14:11–24). God's welcoming embrace, in fact, is available to all humankind. And *there* is the root source of empathy.

In the press, all the media, in the pulpit as well, we hear the call: "Empathy, empathy, empathy!" Does anyone seriously believe that such constant adjuration will have a salutatory effect? Who truly believes that if we double up our fists, tighten our jaws, and determine to become more empathic in our life and our caring and in our prayers we will achieve our goal? I suggest, instead, that such moralizing with oneself in the imperative may, in fact, get in the way of our actually experiencing the real thing. The source of what Barrett Browning called the "Real," in empathy, as in everything else, is not to be found in ourselves, in our competence as willful beings. It is to be found in God's self disclosure, self-revelation,

5. Farmer, *Servant of the Word*, 63.

God's self-giving in Jesus Christ. Jesus Christ is God's radical, divine empathy incarnate. We read of it in the book of Philippians where Paul speaks of the mind of Christ that we have, in Christ Jesus:

> Who, though he was in the form
>   of God,
>   did not regard equality with
>   God
>   as something to be exploited,
> but emptied himself,
>   taking the form of a slave,
>   being born in human likeness.
> And being found in human form,
>   he humbled himself
>   and became obedient to the
>   point of death—
>   even death on a cross.
>
> Therefore God also highly
>   exalted him,
>   and gave him the name
>   that is above every name,
> so that at the name of Jesus
>   every knee should bend
>   in heaven and on earth and
>   under the earth,
> and every tongue should confess,
>   that Jesus Christ is Lord,
>   to the glory of God the Father (Phil 2:5–11).

Please note that the text of Paul's gospel proclamation itself is poetry, hymnody, start to finish. It is theology and art for faith's sake. The radical source, the at-the-root spring or cause of true empathy, is not in ourselves, in our capacity to will it for ourselves. Quite to the contrary, it is to be found in the author of the "Real," the one "through whom all things came into being, and without [whom] not one thing came into being" (John 1:3). If in our artistic efforts, and if in our life together, true empathic, real engagement with lives actual and virtual is to occur, its occurrence will be brought about by Christ indwelling us and all our attempts to bear witness to life as it is, and as it is to become, in him. Paul expresses this truth, especially as it relates to himself, with startling clarity. He says:

> I have been crucified with Christ;
> and it is no longer I who live, but
> it is Christ who lives in me. And
> the life I now live in the flesh
> I live *by the faith of the Son of God*,
> who loved me and gave himself
> for me (Gal 2:19b–20).

To sum up: all attempts at a witness to life in preaching, poetry, prose, and opera entail a giving of life for life. As earlier pointed out, "witness," in the Greek New Testament, is *martyrdom*. It is a giving of life for life in the power of the Spirit.

Bibliography

Achtemeier, Elizabeth. *Preaching as Theology and Art*. Nashville: Abingdon, 1984.

Akhmatova, Anna. "Requiem 1935–1940." In *A Book of Women Poets from Antiquity to Now*, edited by Aliki Barnstone and Willis Barnstone, 378. New York: Shochen, 1980.

Baillie, John. *A Diary of Private Prayer*. New York: Simon and Schuster, 1948.

Barth, Karl. *The Humanity of God*. Richmond, VA: John Knox, 1960.

Bartow, Charles L. "Commentary on Romans 8:19–21." In *The Lectionary Commentary: Theological Exegesis for Sunday's Texts. The Second Readings: Acts and Epistles*, edited by Roger E. van Harn, 164–69. Grand Rapids: Eerdmans, 2001.

———. *God's Human Speech: A Practical Theology of Proclamation*. Grand Rapids: Eerdmans, 1997.

———. *The Preaching Moment: A Guide to Sermon Delivery*. Nashville: Abingdon, 1980.

Bartow, Ernest Winfield. "Prophet in the Pew: Introduction into a Contemporary Style of Christian Proclamation." Unpublished ThM thesis, Princeton Theological Seminary, 1967.

Bates, Katharine Lee. "America the Beautiful." In *The Hymnbook*, edited by David Hugh Jones, Hymn 510. New York: John Ribble, 1955.

Book of Confessions. Louisville: Presbyterian Church (U.S.A.), 1994.

Browning, Elizabeth Barrett. "How Do I Love Thee!" In *Immortal Poems of the English Language*, edited by Oscar Williams, 349. New York: Washington Square, 1952.

———. "The Dead Pan." In *The Complete Works of Elizabeth Barrett Browning*, edited by Horace E. Scudder, 191. Boston: Houghton Mifflin, 1900.

Browning, Robert. "Andrea Del Sarto." In *Selections from The Poetical Works of Robert Browning*, 77. New York: Thomas Y. Crowell, 1886.

Buttrick, George A., ed. *The Interpreter's Bible*. Vol. 7. Nashville: Abingdon, 1951.

Calvin, John. *Institutes of the Christian Religion*. Edited by John T. McNeill. Translated by Ford Lewis Battles. Philadelphia: Westminster, 1960.

Campbell, Strother A. *Grit to Grapple with Life*. Nashville: Broadman, 1942.

Crosby, Fanny Jane. "Blessed Assurance, Jesus Is Mine." In *Glory to God: The Presbyterian Hymnal*, Hymn 839. Louisville: Westminster John Knox, 2013.

Davis, John D., and Henry S. Gehman. *The Westminster Dictionary of the Bible*. Philadelphia: Westminster, 1944.

Dillenberger, John. *Martin Luther: Selections from His Writings*. Garden City, NY: Doubleday, 1961.

Dowey, Edward A., Jr. *The Knowledge of God in Calvin's Theology*. Grand Rapids: Eerdmans, 1994.

Farmer, H. H. *The Servant of the Word*. Philadelphia: Fortress, 1964.

Fosdick, Harry Emerson. "The Forgiveness of Sins." In *Riverside Sermons*, 297. New York: Harper and Brothers, 1958.

Frost, Robert. "The Figure a Poem Makes." In *Complete Poems of Robert Frost*, 49. New York: Henry Holt, 1949.

Gossip, Arthur John. "But When Life Tumbles In, What Then?" In *The Protestant Pulpit*, edited by Andrew Waterson Blackwood, 198. Nashville: Abingdon Cokesbury, 1947.

Guite, Malcomb. *Faith, Hope, and Poetry: Theology and the Poetic Imagination*. Burlington: Ashgate, 2010.

Handel, George F. *The Messiah*. New York: G. Shirmer, 1912.

Hart, David Bentley. *The Beauty of the Infinite: The Aesthetics of Christian Truth*. Grand Rapids: Eerdmans, 2004.

Hinderliter, Harold Horace. "Biblical Interpretation and Historical Method: An Analysis of the Writings of C. H. Dodd, H. H. Farmer, and Alan Richardson." PhD diss., Vanderbilt University, 1960.

Hone, Joseph. *W. B. Yeats*. New York: Macmillan, 1943.

Hughes, Langston. "Mother to Son." In *American Negro Poetry*, edited by Arna Bontemps, 67. New York: Hill and Wang, 1963.

Hunsinger, George. "Commentary on Romans 14:1–12." In *The Lectionary Commentary: Theological Exegesis for Sunday's Texts. The Second Readings: Acts and Epistles*, edited by Roger E. van Harn, 41. Grand Rapids: Eerdmans, 2001.

Kay, James F. *Christus Praesens: A Reconsideration of Rudolf Bultmann's Christology*. Grand Rapids: Eerdmans, 1994.

King, Martin Luther, Jr. "Speech at Illinois Wesleyan University 1966." Recorded Feb. 10, 1966. https://www.iwu.edu/mlk/.

Knapp, Shepherd. "Lord God of Hosts, Whose Purpose, Never Swerving." In *The Hymnbook*, edited by David Hugh Jones, Hymn 288. Philadelphia: John Ribble, 1955.

Langer, Susanne K. *Feeling and Form: A Theory of Art*. New York: Charles Scribner's Sons, 1953.

Lowell, James Russell. "Once to Every Man and Nation." In *The Hymnbook*, edited by David Hugh Jones, Hymn 361. Philadelphia: John Ribble, 1955.

Neumark, George. "If Thou but Suffer God to Guide Thee." translated by Catherine Winkworth. In *The Hymnbook*, edited by David Hugh Jones, Hymn 344. Philadelphia: John Ribble, 1954.

"Nobody Knows the Trouble I've Seen." In *The New American Songbook*, edited by Mark and Ann Oberndorfer. Chicago: Hall and McCreary, 1941.

Ramm, Bernard L. *The Right, the Good, and the Happy.* Waco, TX: Word Books, 1971.

Sayers, Dorothy. "The Zeal of Thy House." In *Religious Drama 1*, edited by Marvin Halverson, 339. New York: The World, 1957.

Scherer, Paul E. "A Prayer." In *Worship Resources for the Christian Year*, edited by Charles L. Wallis, 333. New York: Harper and Brothers, 1954.

————. Unpublished lecture at Princeton Theological Seminary, 1963.

Schmit, Clayton J. "Art for Faith's Sake." *Theology News and Notes* 48:2 (Fall 2001) 3–5.

Shakespeare, William. "Hamlet, Prince of Denmark." In *Shakespeare: The Complete Works*, edited by G. B. Harrison, 906. New York: Harcourt Brace, 1948.

Speer, Robert E. *Five Minutes a Day.* Philadelphia: Westminster, 1943.

Story, Cullen I. K. *The Fourth Gospel: Its Purpose, Pattern, and Power.* Shippensburg, PA: Ragged Edge, 1997.

Tillich, Paul. *Systematic Theology.* Vol. 1. Chicago: The University of Chicago, 1951.

Thomas, Dylan. "Do Not Go Gentle into That Good Night." In *The Collected Poems of Dylan Thomas*, 248. New York: New Directions, 1957.

Yeats, W. B. "The Mother of God." In *The Collected Poems of W. B. Yeats*, edited by Richard J. Finneran, 248. New York: Simon and Schuster, 1996.